がん

GAMBA'RE!

Or

THE JAPANESE WAY
OF THE RUGBY FAN

THE ULTIMATE GUIDE TO JAPAN
AND JAPANESE FOR RUGBY SUPPORTERS

First published 2019 by

G-chan Press
53 Stirling Court
Marshall Street
London W1F 9BD

www.gambare.co.uk

ISBN 9781999359508

Designed and typeset by
Oxford Designers & Illustrators Ltd

Illustrations by Harry Venning

Printed in the UK by Henry Ling Limited

Photo credits

The following photographs are licensed under Creative Commons BY-SA 2.0:

Sukiyaki by nyaa_birdies_perch; teishoku by nakashi; tempura by Norio NAKAYAMA; Teppanyaki by greg; Soup Curry (Supu kare) by oberheim; Hittsumi by Yamamoto Yousuke; Butaman by hirotomo t; Takana-meshi by woinery; Nambu sembei by Roddy McDougall; Abekawa-mochi by Yukiko Yamamoto; Hijoguchi by MIKI Yoshihito; Midori no madoguchi by David McKelvey.

The following photographs are licensed under Creative Commons BY-SA 2.5:

Takoyaki by Keith Perkins; Pollock roe (Mentaiko) by 맛객

The following photographs are licensed under Creative Commons BY-SA 3.0:

Sumidagawa by Rs 1421; Inuyama Castle by ThorstenS; Dazaifu Tenmangu Shrine by 73/Wikimedia commons; Izakaya lantern by jaUser Hykw-a4; Bento by かう;

Konnyaku by Gleam; Nori by Lyzzy; Manju by Ocdp; Natto by Gleam; Ochazuke by Muyo; Okonomiyaki by Naocchi; Sembei by Sakura Midori; Soba by Siriusplot; Nigiri-zushi by (W-T shared) Jpatokal at wts wikivoyage; Tofu by DryPot; Tusukemono by DoWhile; Yakisoba by しんかわな; Inari-zushi, wikmedia user Gogo; Marusei bata sando by Dddeco; Yanagawa nabe by Chris 73/Wikimedia commons; Gyunabe by DangLewis; Tamagoyaki (Akashi-yaki) by ciro; Hakata ramen by Hykw-a4; Mooncake (Geppei) by Fanny Schertzer.

The following photographs are licensed under Creative Commons BY-SA 4.0:

Oden by 松岡明芳; Onigiri by 脇山航; Ramen by Rararamen; Gokabo by Ebiebi 2; Kaminari Okoshi by Kentin; Gaufres (Gofuru) by Jiel Beaumardier; Zabieru by Oitakiseichu.

Creative Commons license wordings are available at https://creativecommons.org/licenses/

Other photographs, etc.:

Yokohama Football Match courtesy of the World Rugby Museum; Sapporo clock tower courtesy of SAPPORO sightseeing photo library; Field near Tono by AMEMAN; Menuma Shōdenzan Kangi-in Temple courtesy of Kumagaya City; Giant Buddha, Kamakura courtesy of Machiga Guide; Dotombori district of Ōsaka courtesy of Machiga Guide; Weathercock House, Kobe courtesy of Kobe Tourism Bureau; Usuki Stone Buddha Statues courtesy of Usuki City; Tendon by Ocdp; Oyakodon by Yamada Taro; Miso-shiru by Hioshi Ishii/flickr; Mochi by Ryosuke Hosei; Sashimi by puamelia/flickr; Shabu-shabu by temaki/flickr; Maki-zushi by cutekirin; Udon by Kyoww; Umeboshi by Batholith; Wagashi by Douglas Perkins; Yakitori by Ocdp; Tamago-fuwafuwa: courtesy of Fukuroi Tourism Association; Vespula (hebo-ryori) by takami torao; Toriten by Toritencat; Kuraun Monaka courtesy of Tsutaya Seikaho; Karashirenkon by Babi Hajau. Eigyochu illustration by きゃらめる; Tachiirikinshi sign at cliff by Nikm.

がんばれ！
GAMBA'RE!

About the authors

Angus Turvill is an award-winning translator of Japanese. His translations include *Tales from a Mountain Cave* by leading humourist Hisashi Inoue, set in and around World-Cup venue *Kamaishi*, with all royalties going to support education and sport in the 2011 *tsunami*-affected community.

Etsuko Okahisa comes from *Naruto* in Japan. She is a highly experienced teacher of Japanese and translation. Her message to rugby fans: 'The people you meet in Japan will be very happy if you try to speak some Japanese! *Gamba're!*'

About the illustrator

Harry Venning is an award-winning cartoonist, illustrator and comedy writer. A weekly contributor to The Guardian with the Clare In The Community strip, his work has also appeared in The Mail On Sunday, Sunday Telegraph, Independent, Sunday Times, The Stage and Radio Times, as well as publications in Canada, Switzerland, South Africa and New Zealand.

Author acknowledgements

The authors would like to express their sincere thanks to the design team at ODI, especially Richard Parker, Carys Evans and Mark Tilley-Watts, to Andrew Cavell, Anne Newman, Freya Gallagher-Jones, Helen Macnaughtan, Jim Baillie, Kana Sakurai, Mike Galbraith and Phil McGowan.

Kon'nichi-wa! Hello!

Welcome to *GAMBA'RE!* – a specially designed guide to Japan and the Japanese language for rugby fans.

GAMBA'RE, like the tea ceremony, cherry blossom and folding shirts neatly, reflects the very essence of Japan – at least for 2019. It means encouragement, perseverance, grit. It is, put simply, Japanese for 'Come on!' – the perfect way to cheer your team to victory!

And fortunately, it can be sung very easily to the tune of the classic upbeat Italian love song 'Volare'. If you think you don't know it, look it up on YouTube.

♫   ♫   ♫

GAMBA'RE oh oh! GAMBA'RE oh oh oh oh!

The book is divided into four sections.

Part 1 (At the stadium) introduces simple language for the rugby fan: opinions on the match, cheering the players on, finding your seat, apologising for stepping on someone's foot, buying a snack, being friendly to people you meet, and questioning the referee's judgement…

Part 2 (What's the score?) is a bracing sprint through Japanese numbers – so that you can forecast even the most optimistic match scores, as well as keep a check on prices.

Part 3 (What does that say?) gives you a way of working out what written language says. It will help you read menus and signs.

Part 4 (What do we do?) Travel is exciting, but it often involves uncertainty, hunger and thirst. To help deal with these, Part 4 contains practical information on key issues facing the traveller: eating and drinking, accommodation, transport, etiquette and so on. It includes essential language for use in restaurants, bars, shops and hotels, as well as in emergencies. It has illustrated guides to Japanese food and venue specialities. It gives information on getting to the venues, as well as suggestions for nearby visits and where to go next.

Throughout the book new information is introduced in numbered sub-sections headed ***ENGAGE!*** Where language elements have been introduced, ***ENGAGE!*** sections are generally followed by practice sessions headed **TRAINING.**

Japanese words are given in Latin alphabet throughout the book. After introduction of the *katakana* syllabary in Part 3, *katakana* is given for all words that are normally written using that script. Other words are given in Japanese script too where this may be helpful for identifying shop signs, etc.

GAMBA'RE!

Notes on the representation of Japanese in Latin alphabet in this book:

1. All Japanese words given in alphabet are written in italics, even if the words are well known in the West.

2. Most long vowels are indicated by the use of macrons. For えい and いい combinations, however, the conventions of using '*ei*' and '*ii*' are followed. Macrons are used even in familiar place names (e.g. *Tōkyō*), to encourage Japanese-style pronunciation.

3. To try to reflect Japanese-style pronunciation accurately, post-vocalic '*n*' (ん) is represented as '*m*' before bilabial plosives '*p*' and '*b*' (e.g. *gamba're*).

4. Where considered helpful, post-vocalic '*n*' (ん) in other mid-word positions is bracketed to suggest that a full English-style '*n*' is not appropriate (e.g. *ki(n)'en.*).

5. Where it is considered helpful, a change of syllable is indicated by use of an apostrophe (e.g. *gamba're*). This is not generally done with names.

6. Hyphens are sometimes used to break up long words into more manageable reading units (e.g. *nigiri-zushi*).

7. The combination of small ッ (*tsu*) plus consonant in Japanese is represented in alphabet as a double consonant in keeping with convention (e.g. *kappu*).

8. Place and personal names are given initial capital letters.

CONTENTS

Warm-up 1 – The Vowel Haka

In a moment we'll go to the stadium, but first let's warm up a little with the Vowel Haka.

Here it is – the Japanese Haka Five – a line-up of pure sounds:

> A as in 'H**a**ka'
> I as in 'w**i**ll'
> U as in 'p**u**sh'
> E as in '**E**ddie'
> O as in '**O**n'

H**a**ka w**i**ll p**u**sh **E**ddie **o**n
A   I   U   E   O

Chant the Haka Five five times with all the feeling you can muster. (If you don't like the idea of pushing Eddie **on**, feel free to chant about pushing him **off**. It's the '**o**' that matters.)

Once you've done that, you pretty much know how to pronounce every vowel in Japanese. Five simple sounds. (That compares to twenty in English!) Okay. Let's make a word from some of those sounds:

A O I   *aoi* = blue

> **Miniquiz 1:** What colour are the French team's shirts?
> Answer in Japanese.

Tensa'i da! You're a genius!

(Essential Japanese for the rugby fan)

Pulse racing? Straining at the leash? Good. Let's go straight into the stadium…get a snack, find our seats and say hello to the person sitting next to us. *What!?!* Come on. Why not? *Gamba're!*

Aims
ENGAGE! 1: Ask where things are
ENGAGE! 2: Buy a snack
ENGAGE! 3: Get to your seat
ENGAGE! 4: Introduce yourself
ENGAGE! 5: Describe match prospects
ENGAGE! 6: Comment on play
ENGAGE! 7: Talk after the match

Difficulty rating ◯◯
Enjoyment rating ◯◯◯◯◯

Don't stand around umming and ahing, wondering who to ask. With just a few words of Japanese you can ask ANYBODY!

> **Sumima'sen!**
> (Excuse me!)
>
> **X wa doko desu ka?**
> (Where is X?)
>
> **Arigatō!**
> (Thank you!)

For example:

> **Sumima'sen!**
> **E retsu wa doko desu ka?** (Where's Row E?)
> **Arigatō!**

Word by word	
E retsu	row E
wa	(topic particle)
doko	where
desu	is (politeness marker)
ka	(question particle)

That's all very well, you may say, but even if I ask I'm not going to understand the other person's reply. **Don't be soft.** There's a limit to what they can say. Here are some simple instructions to listen for:

> *Massugu* (straight ahead)
> *Hidari* (left)
> *Migi* (right)

 Training 1

Use the question pattern to ask where the following things are:

row G	G retsu
toilet	toi're
entrance	iriguchi
exit	deguchi
my seat	watashi no seki
food/drink stand	ba'iten

Remember: every vowel is pronounced as in the Haka Five.
H**a**ka w**i**ll p**u**sh **E**ddie **o**n. A line over a vowel (as in *arigatō*) just makes it a bit longer.

Don't forget to say
Sumima'sen (Excuse me) and **Arigatō** (Thank you)!

(Don't worry about 'the' or 'a'. Japanese has no real equivalent.)

Engage! 2 | Buying a snack

Better get some refreshment before the match. You've successfully found your way to a *ba'iten* (food/drink stand). Now try buying something:

> ### Sumima'sen!
> (Excuse me!)
>
> ### X kudasa'i
> (X please)

For example:
Sumima'sen!
Kōhī kudasa'i. (Coffee, please.)

Training 2

Ask for some of these items at a food/drink stand.

Thank the person who serves you.

sandwich	*sando'icchi* (pronounced: it'chy)
nuts	*nattsu*
rice ball	*onigiri* ('g' pronounced as in 'girl')
ice cream	*a'isu-kurīmu*

coffee	*kōhī*
tea (black)	*kōcha*
tea (green)	*ocha*
water	*mizu*
beer	*bīru*

Engage! 3 | Getting to your seat

From *Engage!* 1 you're already a dab hand at asking where your seat is. But if it's in the middle of the row, you'll have to get past other spectators.

What do you say?

Use the multi-purpose word: **sumima'sen** (very like English 'sorry')

- To ask to get past someone: **sumima'sen**

- If someone stands up to let you pass: **sumima'sen**

- If you tread on someone's foot as you pass along the row:
  sumima'sen

- If you find someone is sitting in your seat:
  sumima'sen, *watashi no seki desu.* (Sorry, that is my seat.)

- If you realise you've made a mistake about that: **sumima'sen**

- Finally, for a bit of variety, if you get there first and someone else is trying to get past **you**, you can say **dōzo** as you squeeze back to let them by. (*Dōzo* is a word used when offering something, or allowing someone to do something.)

Training 3

You have found your row, but your seat is in the middle and everybody else is already sitting down. Get to your seat – in Japanese:

Ask to get past…

Thank somebody for letting you past…

You have trodden on their foot.   Apologise…

You find somebody in your seat.   Tell them it is your seat…

You realise you have made a mistake.   Apologise…

You've finally reached your seat and someone is trying to get past you. You move back and encourage them to go by…

Now you're safely in your seat, why not be friendly and introduce yourself to the Japanese people around you? They'll love it! They'll love you!

To say hello, the expression depends on the time of day:

Good morning!	*ohayō goza'imasu*
Good day!	*kon'nichi-wa*
Good evening!	*komban-wa*

Then give some information about yourself:

> ### X desu.
> (I'm X [name])
>
> ### Y-jin desu
> (I'm Y [nationality])

For example:

    Kon'nichi-wa! (Good day!/Hello!)
    Cathy desu. (I'm Cathy.)
    Sukottorando-jin desu. (I'm Scottish.)

To say your nationality add *-jin* to the Japanese name for your country in the table opposite.

(NB: The word **desu** is normally pronounced **dess**.)

NATIONS

Argentina		Aruzenchin
Australia		Ōsutoraria
Britain		Igirisu
Canada		Kanada
England		Ingurando
Fiji		Fijī
France		Furansu
Georgia		Jōjia
Ireland		A'irurando
Italy		Itaria
Japan		Nihon/Nippon
Namibia		Namibia
New Zealand		Nyūjīrando
Russia		Roshia
Samoa		Samoa
Scotland		Sukottorando
South Africa		Minami-afurika
Tonga		Tonga
USA		Amerika
Uruguay		Urugua'i
Wales		Wēruzu

That's enough about you. Now introduce your companions. For example:

> **John *desu.***
> (This is John.)
>
> ***Otto desu.***
> (He's my husband.)

(Obviously there may be confusion if you are with a friend called Otto.)

Here are some other words you might want to use. Just add *desu* after the word: e.g. *otōsan desu*. This/He is my father.

RELATIONSHIPS	
father	*otōsan*
mother	*okāsan*
child	*kodomo*
daughter	*musu'me*
son	*musuko*
brother	*onīsan* (older brother) *otōto* (younger brother)
sister	*onēsan* (older sister) *imōto* (younger sister)
husband	*otto*
wife	*tsuma*
uncle	*ojisan*
aunt	*obasan*
nephew	*oi*
niece	*mei*
grandchild	*mago*
grandfather	*ojīsan*
grandmother	*obāsan*
cousin	*itoko*
friend	*tomodachi*

Training 4

This is *Aiko* (*A'iko*), in the next seat. She's very friendly, but she doesn't speak a word of English. So speak to her in Japanese.

" Say hello ...
Say your name ...
Say your nationality ...

Introduce your companion:

Say their name ...
Say their relationship to you ... "

Engage! 5 | Match prospects

Everyone wants to give an opinion on their team's prospects before a match starts. Here are seven alternatives ranging from a high level of confidence to stoic acceptance of fate:

We'll win	*katsu darō* ☺
It's going to be close	*sessen ni narisō*
It's going to be tough	*muzukashii* 😐
It's going to be very tough	*kiwa'me'te muzukashii*
We may lose	*ma'keru kamo*
Well, I suppose we'll lose	*mā...ma'keru darō* ☹

Putting a bit more feeling into it:

| We're going to win! | *katsu ze!* |
| We're going to win! (Cute – not recommended for self-identifying alpha males.) | *katsu wa!* |

Training 5

1. Your team is playing against Japan. How do you feel about your team's prospects?

   a) ☺   b) 😐   c) ☹

   Put your feelings into words (Japanese words).

2. If you win against Japan, you're playing New Zealand. How do you rate your chances? Answer in Japanese.

Of course, you may be from New Zealand yourself. In that case before answering question 2, why not take this opportunity of looking at the world through others' eyes? Choose a new nationality from the list on p.17.

Nobody wants a silent crowd. So learn to let your emotions out in Japanese. Shout, cheer, yell, mutter, sigh, groan!

Positive/encouraging

Gamba're! (Come on!)	
I'ke, i'ke! (Go! Go!)	
O'se, O'se! (Push! Push!)	
Ii zo, ii zo! (It's going well! Great work!)	
Mō hito'iki! (Keep going! One last effort!)	
Haya'i! (He's/They're quick!)	Try adapting this to the local dialect, depending on where you are in Japan: *Hayē!* (eastern Japan) *Haya!* (western Japan)
Sugoi! (Amazing!)	Or in local dialect: *Sugē!* (eastern Japan) *Sugo!* (western Japan)
[TEAM/PLAYER/POSITION] *wa tsuyoi ne!* ([TEAM/NAME/POSITION] is/are good, isn't he/aren't they.)	
Tora'i da! (It's a try!)	Caution! If you try localising *tora'i* in the same way as *haya'i* and *sugoi*, you may find yourself shouting about tigers: *Tora da!* It's a tiger! Or even trays: *Torē da!* It's a tray!

Negative/critical

Osoi! (He's/They're slow!)	Or in local dialect: *Osē!* (eastern Japan) *Oso!* (western Japan)
Mō da'me da! (It's no use!/It's too late!)	
Hansoku da! (That's a foul!)	
Notto-sutrēto da! (Not straight!)	
Referī mi'te na'i yo! (The referee's not looking!)	

Here are more rugby words you might want to use. A lot of them will look familiar, but pronunciation is key. Always remember the Vowel Haka! (p. 10)

POSITIONS	
prop	*puroppu*
lock	*rokku*
hooker	*fukkā*
flanker	*furankā*
number eight	*nambā-eito*
scrum half	*sukuramu-hāfu*
fly half	*fura'i-hāfu*
centre	*sentā*
wing	*u'ingu*
full back	*furu-bakku*

UMPIRING

referee	*re'ferī*
touch judge	*tacchi-jajji*
whistle	*fu'e*
flag	*hata*

MATCH

X versus Y	*X ta'i Y*
first half	*ze(n)han*
second half	*kōhan*
half time	*hāfu-ta'imu*
stoppage time	*rosu-ta'imu*

ACTION

pass	*pasu suru*
kick	*kikku suru*
tackle	*takkuru suru*
run	*hashiru*
push	*osu*
drop (the ball)	*otosu*
scrum	*sukuramu*
line out	*ra'in-a'uto*
ruck	*rakku*
maul	*mōru*

SCORE	
try	tora'i
goal	gōru
conversion	kombāshon
drop goal	doroppu-gōru
penalty goal	penarutī-gōru
points	ten

FOULS	
foul	hansoku
dangerous tackle	ki'ken na takkuru
knock on	nokku-on
not straight	notto-sutorēto
throw forward	surō-fowādo
off side	ofu-sa'ido
penalty kick	penarutī-kikku
free kick	furī-kikku

ON AND OFF THE PITCH	
send off	ta'ijō
sin bin	shimbin
substitute	kōta'i
injury	fushō

TOURNAMENT	
pool	pūru
quarter-final	jun-jun-kesshō
semi-final	jun-kesshō
final	kesshō

For names of nations see p. 17.

Say/shout/mumble the following in Japanese:

> *Come on!*
> *Push! Push!*
> *It's going well!*
> *He's quick!*
> *Amazing!*
> *That's a foul!*
> *The referee's not looking!*

Engage! 7 | After the match

You may not manage a full Japanese blow-by-blow post-match analysis, but you'll be able to communicate. Here are a few simple comments.

Katta! (We won!)
Yattā! (Great!)
Yoku yatta! They did well!

Ma'keta! (We lost!)
Zannen datta! (That's a pity!)
Shōgana'i! (Can't be helped!)

Hikiwa'ke (A draw)
Sessen datta ne! (It was close, wasn't it!)

Omoshiro-katta! (It was good/fun!)
Ta'ikutsu datta! (It was boring!)

Ka'erō! (Let's go home!)

 Training 7

Say the following in Japanese:

> **We won!**
> **Great!**
> **It was close, wasn't it!**
> **It was fun!**
> **Let's go home!**

That's the end of Part 1

Ii zo, ii zo! (You're doing well!)

Warm-up 2 – *Motto* Vowel Haka

Remember the Vowel Haka?

> Haka wi**ll** p**u**sh **E**ddie **o**n
> A I U E O

Let's add in some consonants. We'll try K first. Chant the vowels on their own, then with K in front:

A I U E O	KA KI KU KE KO

Here's a word using the syllables you've just chanted:

A KA I *aka'i* = red

Let's try some more consonants. The vowels stay the same:

SA	SHI	SU	SE	SO		TA	CHI	TSU	TE	TO
NA	NI	NU	NE	NO		HA	HI	FU	HE	HO
MA	MI	MU	ME	MO		RA	RI	RU	RE	RO

Here are some more words. Say them out loud.

TO RA I   SU KU RA MU

What do they mean?   (Answers on p. 151)

> **Miniquiz 2:** What colour are the Welsh team's shirts?
> Answer in Japanese.

Sugoi! Amazing!

(Japanese numbers)

If you can say the score in Japanese, you'll be a hero in Japan! And it's always best to know how much you're being charged. So let's get a grip on numbers. You'll enjoy it!

Aims
ENGAGE! 8: Numbers 0–10   Saying the score.
ENGAGE! 9: Numbers 11–19
ENGAGE! 10: Numbers 20–99
ENGAGE! 11: Numbers 100–1,000,000
ENGAGE! 12: How much?   Currencies; prices.

Difficulty rating ◌
Enjoyment rating ◌◌◌◌◌

All set? We'll start with 0 (nil). Nil is *rei* – as in *ray of hope*.

Having learnt 'nothing' in the first line, let's try 1 to 10. That's not overdoing it, is it? A bit of concentration and they'll be tripping off your tongue in no time. Here goes:

Look at the images and say the words:

1 *ichi* itchy	**2 *ni*** knee
3 *san* sun ('sun' and 'san' sound the same in Japanese)	**4 *yon*** yawn (the vowel's a bit shorter than 'yawn' really – like '**yon**der')
5 *go* ready, steady, **go** (the vowel's a bit shorter than 'go' really – like **go**lf)	**6 *roku*** lock (or rock) ('l' and 'r' sound the same in Japanese)
7 *nana* banana ('*na*' as in 'nap')	**8 *hachi*** hatch
9 *kyū* queue	**10 *jū*** juice

Now say them again, miming the actions:

1 ichi Scratch yourself	**2 ni** Point to your knee
3 san Point to the sun	**4 yon** Yawn
5 go Start running	**6 roku** Lock the door
7 nana Eat a banana	**8 hachi** Chick hatching
9 kyū Stand in a queue	**10 jū** Drink some juice

Once more: say the Japanese numbers and mime the related actions (as you did on the previous page):

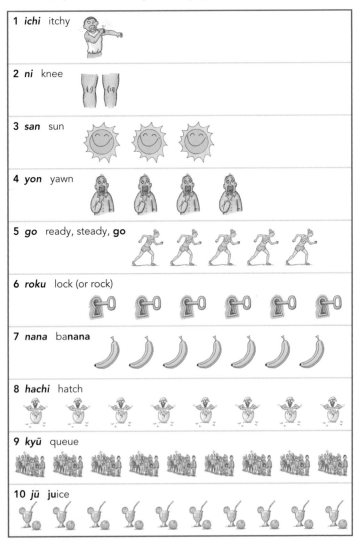

1 *ichi* itchy

2 *ni* knee

3 *san* sun

4 *yon* yawn

5 *go* ready, steady, **go**

6 *roku* lock (or rock)

7 *nana* banana

8 *hachi* hatch

9 *kyū* queue

10 *jū* juice

Look at the pictures and say numbers 1–10 in Japanese:

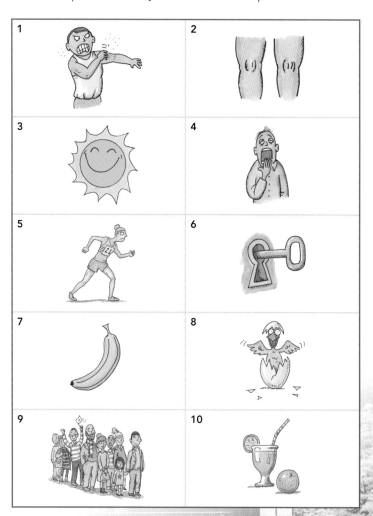

 Training 8 (b)

Say these numbers in Japanese, miming the related actions as previously:

1	2	3	4
5	6	7	8
9	10		

Now say these numbers:

5	3	8	7
10	6	2	1
4	9		

And once more for luck. (If you don't remember 0, see p. 30)

3	7	1	6
8	9	10	4
5	2	0	

What's the score? *Nan ta'i nani*? (literally: what versus what?)

When saying the score between two teams you say (NUMBER) *ta'i* (NUMBER).

Say the following scores in Japanese:

a) 5–3 (example: **go ta'i san**)

b) 10–0

c) 8–7

d) 0–6

e) 9–5

(Answers on p. 151)

Once you've mastered 0 to 10 there's no stopping you.
What comes next couldn't be simpler.

(10 *jū*)	11 *jū-ichi*
12 *jū-ni*	13 *jū-san*
14 *jū-yon*	15 *jū-go*
16 *jū-roku*	17 *jū-nana*
18 *jū-hachi*	19 *jū-kyū*

As you can see from the table, for 11 to 19 just take the Japanese
for ten (*jū*) and add the other numbers as necessary:

   11 = *jū-ichi*: *jū* (ten) + *ichi* (one)
   12 = *jū-ni*: *jū* (ten) + *ni* (two) … and so on

 Training 9

Say these scores in Japanese:

a) 3–17 (example: *san ta'i jū-nana*)

b) 16–10

c) 8–14

d) 15–11

e) 19–0

(Answers on p. 151)

There's nothing complicated here. The numbers 20–99 are shown in the chart for reference, with a few comments beneath.

20 *ni-jū*	30 *san-jū*	40 *yon-jū*	50 *go-jū*	60 *roku-jū*	70 *nana-jū*	80 *hachi-jū*	90 *kyū-jū*
21 *ni-jū-ichi*	31 *san-jū-ichi*	41 *yon-jū-ichi*	51 *go-jū-ichi*	61 *roku-jū-ichi*	71 *nana-jū-ichi*	81 *hachi-jū-ichi*	91 *kyū-jū-ichi*
22 *ni-jū-ni*	32 *san-jū-ni*	42 *yon-jū-ni*	52 *go-jū-ni*	62 *roku-jū-ni*	72 *nana-jū-ni*	82 *hachi-jū-ni*	92 *kyū-jū-ni*
23 *ni-jū-san*	33 *san-jū-san*	43 *yon-jū-san*	53 *go-jū-san*	63 *roku-jū-san*	73 *nana-jū-san*	83 *hachi-jū-san*	93 *kyū-jū-san*
24 *ni-jū-yon*	34 *san-jū-yon*	44 *yon-jū-yon*	54 *go-jū-yon*	64 *roku-jū-yon*	74 *nana-jū-yon*	84 *hachi-jū-yon*	94 *kyū-jū-yon*
25 *ni-jū-go*	35 *san-jū-go*	45 *yon-jū-go*	55 *go-jū-go*	65 *roku-jū-go*	75 *nana-jū-go*	85 *hachi-jū-go*	95 *kyū-jū-go*
26 *ni-jū-roku*	36 *san-jū-roku*	46 *yon-jū-roku*	56 *go-jū-roku*	66 *roku-jū-roku*	76 *nana-jū-roku*	86 *hachi-jū-roku*	96 *kyū-jū-roku*
27 *ni-jū-nana*	37 *san-jū-nana*	47 *yon-jū-nana*	57 *go-jū-nana*	67 *roku-jū-nana*	77 *nana-jū-nana*	87 *hachi-jū-nana*	97 *kyū-jū-nana*
28 *ni-jū-hachi*	38 *san-jū-hachi*	48 *yon-jū-hachi*	58 *go-jū-hachi*	68 *roku-jū-hachi*	78 *nana-jū-hachi*	88 *hachi-jū-hachi*	98 *kyū-jū-hachi*
29 *ni-jū-kyū*	39 *san-jū-kyū*	49 *yon-jū-kyū*	59 *go-jū-kyū*	69 *roku-jū-kyū*	79 *nana-jū-kyū*	89 *hachi-jū-kyū*	99 *kyū-jū-kyū*

Look at the top line of the table on the previous page and you'll see that 20, 30, 40, etc. work in the most logical way possible:

20: *ni-jū* (2 x 10)

30: *san-jū* (3 x 10)

40: *yon-jū* (4 x 10), etc.

Look at the next lines and you'll see that intermediate numbers work in the same way as English:

21: *ni-jū-ichi* (20 + 1)

22: *ni-jū-ni* (20 + 2)…and so on, right up to 99.

 Training 10

Say these scores in Japanese:

a) 40–16 (example: *yon-jū ta'i jū-roku*)

b) 25–7

c) 3–88

d) 32–9

e) 50–15 (Answers on p. 151)

> **Miniquiz 3**
> What was the score in the 2015 World Cup Final between New Zealand and Australia?
>
> a) *Ni-jū-go ta'i jū-roku*
>
> b) *San-jū-yon ta'i jū-nana*
>
> c) *San-jū-roku ta'i ni-jū-kyū* (Answer on p. 151)

You can now count up to 99. Fantastic! But does it cover every possible score? Perhaps not. We'd better go a step further. *Hyaku* (100) should do the trick. 101 is just **hyaku-ichi** and so on.

> **Miniquiz 4**
> What is the highest ever score by a team in a World Cup match?
>
> a) *hachi-jū-ni*   b) *hyaku-yon-jū-go*   c) *hyaku-jū-yon*
>
> (Answer on p. 151)

I think that's scores sorted out. But what about money? A hundred yen can get you some quite interesting items in a 'hyaku-en shoppu' (100-yen shop), but it's not going to go far anywhere else. Your wallet's going to be haemorrhaging thousands of yen every day.

So to let you keep track of prices, we're going to go higher, right up to a million. Here's the basic information:

1. Hundreds

100	hyaku
200	ni-hyaku
300	**sambyaku**
400	yon-hyaku
500	go-hyaku
600	**roppyaku**
700	nana-hyaku
800	**happyaku**
900	kyū-hyaku

Simple enough: *ni* (two) + *hyaku* (hundred) (*ni-hyaku*) and so on. But note there's a little variation when it comes to 300, 600 and 800.

For numbers between the hundreds, just add on the relevant smaller number: 201 = *ni-hyaku-ichi*; 202 = *ni-hyaku-ni*, etc.

2. 1,000–9,999

1,000	sen
2,000	ni-sen
3,000	**sanzen**
4,000	yon-sen
5,000	go-sen
6,000	roku-sen
7,000	nana-sen
8,000	**hassen**
9,000	kyū-sen

Again, straightforward, but with slight irregularity for 3,000 and 8,000.

For numbers between the thousands, again, just add on the relevant smaller number: 2,001 = ni-sen-ichi; 2,002 = ni-sen-ni

3. 10,000 +

Things are slightly different once you reach 10,000.

In Japanese '10,000' is a unit in itself, known as man. So 10,000 is ichi-man (one ten-thousand), 20,000 is ni-man (two ten-thousands), etc. This carries on through 100,000 (jū-man – ten ten-thousands) and a million (hyaku-man – a hundred ten-thousands).

10,000	ichi-man
20,000	ni-man
30,000	san-man
40,000	yon-man
50,000	go-man
60,000	roku-man
70,000	nana-man
80,000	hachi-man
90,000	kyū-man
100,000	jū-man
1,000,000	hyaku-man

Engage! 12 | How much?

Okay. Hundreds, thousands, millions – you now know them all. With this wad of numerical knowledge up your sleeve, you're ready to face the critical question.

> ### Ikura desu ka?
> (How much is it?)

Word by word	
ikura	how much
desu	is (politeness marker)
ka	(question particle)

The answer will, of course, be a number + currency name, usually **en** (yen).

English currency name	Japanese currency name
yen	*en*
dollar	*doru*
pound	*pondo*
euro	*yūro*
rand	*rando*

Example amounts: ¥1,000 – *sen-en*;   €20 – *ni-jū-yūro*

 Training 12

1. Match the prices on the left and right:

   a) ¥300
   b) ¥650
   c) ¥3,000
   d) ¥5,210
   e) ¥25,000
   f) ¥30,000
   g) ¥340,000

   i)   *san-man-en*
   ii) *go-sen-ni-hyaku-jū-en*
   iii) *roppyaku-go-jū-en*
   iv) *san-jū-yon-man-en*
   v)   *ni-man-go-sen-en*
   vi) *san-zen-en*
   vii) *sambyaku-en*

   (Answers on p. 151)

2. Look at the exchange rates and answer the questions in Japanese:

Currency Exchange 両替 (ryōga'e)	
Aus *doru*	¥83
NZ *doru*	¥76
US *doru*	¥112
Pondo	¥149
Yūro	¥132
Rando	¥9

(exchange rates from mid-2018) (zero commission)

   a) £100 *(hyaku-pondo)* wa en de **ikura desu ka**?
      (How much is £100 in yen?)
   b) NZ$1,000 *(sen-doru)* wa en de **ikura desu ka**?
      (How much is NZ$1,000 in yen?)

(Answers on p. 151)

Minquiz 5: What is the official price of:

a) The cheapest World Cup tickets?

b) The most expensive World Cup tickets?

Answer in Japanese.

(Answers on p. 151)

That's the end of Part 2

Yoku yatta! (You've done well!)

Warm-up 3 – *Motto Motto* Vowel Haka

Okay, time for more chanting. You're doing really well, so we'll throw in a few more consonants this time.

A	I	U	E	O		KA	KI	KU	KE	KO
SA	SHI	SU	SE	SO		TA	CHI	TSU	TE	TO
NA	NI	NU	NE	NO		HA	HI	FU	HE	HO
MA	MI	MU	ME	MO		RA	RI	RU	RE	RO
GA	GI	GU	GE	GO		ZA	JI	ZU	ZE	ZO
BA	BI	BU	BE	BO		PA	PI	PU	PE	PO

Let's make a word from what you've just chanted. Take the following syllables: RA GU BI. Make the vowel in BI longer: BĪ. And there it is: RA GU BĪ. Sound familiar? Say it just like that – three syllables, the last with a long 'i': *ragubī*.

(Note: Japanese doesn't distinguish between the vowels in 'rug' and 'rag'.)

Long vowels are important. Say the following place names making the vowels long where shown (ō/ū)

Tōkyō	*Ōsaka*	*Kōbe*	*Ōita*
Hokkaidō	*Honshū*	*Kyūshū*	

We'll deal with double consonants here too – as in *Ho**kk**aidō*. Think of the first of the two consonants as a silent beat. So in *Ho**kk**aidō* the first *k* is a very brief silence before the following *ka* sound: *Ho()kaidō*

PART 3 | What does that say?

(Deciphering Japanese words)

ガンバレ
オオ
ガンバレ
オオオオ

When you get to Japan you'll be surrounded by strange-looking script. There'll be a sprinkling of alphabet too, but beyond the airport arrivals hall a lot of that is just decoration. As for the Japanese, you won't be able to understand a word. Or so you'd think… but in fact, with the support of Part 3 and a little commitment you'll be able to decipher some of this script quite quickly. So keep reading! *Gamba're!*

Aims
ENGAGE! 13: Get to know the types of Japanese script
ENGAGE! 14–16: Learn to decipher *katakana*
ENGAGE! 17: Recognise *kanji* for venue names in Japanese

Difficulty rating ◯◯◯◯
Enjoyment rating ◯◯◯◯◯

Engage! 13 | Japanese script

A bit of background first:

Q: What types of script are there in Japanese?

A: *Kanji* characters, the *hiragana* syllabary and the *katakana* syllabary.

Here is the word *Nihon* (Japan) written in each of the scripts:

日本　(*kanji*)

にほん (*hiragana*)

ニホン (*katakana*)

1. *Kanji* characters. (漢字)

Originating in China, there are thousands of *kanji* characters in Japanese. They can look complicated and they often have multiple readings. They're also fascinating. 日, the first of the characters in 日本 above, can be read '*ni*', '*nichi*' or '*hi*', depending on context. It is used to mean 'Japan', 'the sun' and 'day'. The second of the characters, 本, can be read '*hon*' or '*moto*' and is used to mean 'book' and 'origin'. So in terms of meaning, we can read 日本 as sun origin – or land of the rising sun.

We could go on talking about *kanji* till the cows come home. But time is limited. In preparation for the World Cup the focus of our *kanji* training will be the characters used in the venue names. See *Engage!* 17.

2. *Hiragana* (ひらがな) and *katakana* (カタカナ)

Hiragana and *katakana* were developed in Japan and both represent the same sounds; but they look different and are used in different ways.

Hiragana is the more rounded of the two, appearance-wise. You'll see it mixed with *kanji* in signs, menus, advertisements and newspapers. Like the cement between bricks, *hiragana* is often what links (grammatically) one *kanji* word to another. But it can also

be used in place of *kanji* words. You'll see it on railway platforms, where the name of the station is always written in *hiragana* as well as in *kanji*. Fortunately for foreign visitors, it is normally written in alphabet too. *Hiragana* is the script used for the title on the front of this book: **がんばれ** (*gamba're*).

Katakana, the more angular of the two syllabaries, is the one we're really going to concentrate on. It's *katakana* that is used to write words borrowed from Western languages. There are thousands of such words in Japanese – including words for Western foods, drinks and sport. *Katakana* is how rugby terms are written, as well as the names of World Cup teams and players. If you can decipher the *katakana* characters, you're very likely to be able to work out what the word means. You won't always be able to, but quite often you will.

Engage! 14–16 show you how to decipher *katakana*. The charts and related materials used in these sections are summarised in Appendix 4 (p. 153–4) on a single page (back and front) in case you want to cut it out for ready reference.

In the warm-ups you've been chanting groups of syllables which share the same basic vowels – the Haka Five (p. 10). The chart below shows how these syllables appear in *katakana*.

Katakana: The basic 45 symbols

Vowels	ア A	イ I	ウ U	エ E	オ O	
K	カ KA	キ KI	ク KU	ケ KE	コ KO	
S	サ SA	シ SHI	ス SU	セ SE	ソ SO	
T	タ TA	チ CHI	ツ TSU	テ TE	ト TO	
N	ナ NA	ニ NI	ヌ NU	ネ NE	ノ NO	Post-vocalic ン N
H	ハ HA	ヒ HI	フ FU	ヘ HE	ホ HO	
M	マ MA	ミ MI	ム MU	メ ME	モ MO	
Y	ヤ YA		ユ YU		ヨ YO	
R(L)*	ラ RA	リ RI	ル RU	レ RE	ロ RO	
W	ワ WA					

*NB: No distinction is made between R and L in Japanese.

You'll see that while most of these syllables require two letters of the alphabet, in *katakana* they are represented by a single symbol. So, for example, KA, two letters in alphabet, becomes the single character カ in *katakana* (column 2, line 2).

Let's read some words using this chart:

1. Look at the vowels in the top line of the chart. Find ア, オ and イ. See what sounds they represent. Read them together as a single word アオイ. What does the word mean? (Hint: you may remember from Warm-up 1, p. 10.)

2. Look also at the K group of syllables on the second line. On these first and second lines find ア, カ and イ. Read them together as a single word. What does it mean? (Hint: you may remember from Warm-up 2, p. 28.)

3. Now look down the second column from the left and find these characters: カ,タ,カ,ナ. Read them together as a single word. (Hint: it's one type of Japanese writing! See the top of p.48.)

NB: Some of the *katakana* characters are difficult to distinguish at first. This is especially true of the following pairs:

シ (*shi*) and ツ (*tsu*)

ン (*n*) and ソ (*so*)

To differentiate シ (*shi*) and ツ (*tsu*), note that the strokes in the character シ (*shi*) are slightly more horizontal than those in ツ (*tsu*), and that the longest stroke is thickest at the bottom in シ (*shi*) and at the top in ツ (*tsu*). The thicker parts are where the writer starts the stroke – at the top in ツ (*tsu*) and at the bottom in シ (*shi*).

Compare ン (*n*) and ソ (*so*). Look for the same types of difference as between シ (*shi*) and ツ (*tsu*).

 Training 14

Referring to the chart on p. 48:

1) Which of these words means 'scrum'?

   a) スカンク   b) スキム   c) スクラム

2) Which of these words means 'try'?

   a) トレイ   b) トライ   c) トイレ

3) Which of these words refers to a rugby set-piece?

   a) ライムライト   b) ラインアウト   c) ラインラント

(Answers on p. 151–2)

On p. 48 we looked at the 45 basic *katakana* characters. In their basic form these 45 represent one syllable each. But Japanese uses more than 100 different syllables. To represent these in *katakana*, there are a number of variations that can be applied to the basic characters:

Variation 1

Two small strokes (like speech marks) at top-right of characters. This changes the pronunciation as follows:

K to G – for example: **カ** (KA) becomes **ガ** (GA), **キ** (KI) becomes **ギ** (GI) and so on.

S to Z – for example: **サ** (SA) becomes **ザ** (ZA), etc.

SH to J – **シ** (SHI) becomes **ジ** (JI)

T to D – for example: **タ** (TA) becomes **ダ** (DA), etc.

TS to Z – **ツ** (TSU) becomes **ヅ** (ZU)

H to B – for example: **ハ** (HA) becomes **バ** (BA), etc.

F to B – **フ** (FU) becomes **ブ** (BU)

U to VU – **ウ** (U) becomes **ヴ** (VU)

Variation 2

A **small circle** top-right of an H (or F) character changes the sound to P:

For example: **ハ** (HA) becomes **パ** (PA), etc.

フ (FU) becomes **プ** (PU).

Variation 3

A **long horizontal stroke** after any character lengthens the vowel:

For example: **ボ** is BO. Add a horizontal stroke like this : **ボー** and pronunciation is BŌ. Example: **ボール** BŌ RU = *bōru* = ball.

Variation 4

A **small ツ (TSU)** character signifies a short pause before the following consonant:

For example: **キック** KI (PAUSE) KU = *kikku* = kick.

(As mentioned in Warm-up 3 (p. 44), when writing in alphabet the pause is represented by the doubling of the next consonant – in this example: *ki<u>kk</u>u*.)

Variation 5

Combining two characters – a character in full-sized font followed by another character in smaller font. This changes the vowel of the full-sized character.

We'll give examples of variations 1–4 here. Variation 5 will be looked at in *Engage!* 16.

Here are examples of words with variations 1–4. We're going to read the words in turn:

Variation 1 Example
Word: **トンガ**

Find each of the symbols **ト**, **ン**, and **ガ** in the chart on p. 48 and see if any variations apply.

ト Column 6, line 4. No variation. Reading: TO

ン Column 7, line 5: Post-vocalic N. No variation. Reading: N

ガ The basic form is in Column 2, line 2: **カ** (KA). But to the top-right of the symbol are two small strokes, as described in variation 1 (p. 50). This changes the K to G. So the reading is GA.

So the full word is TO N GA = *tonga* = Tonga.

Variation 2 Example
Word: **パス**

Find each of the symbols, **パ** and **ス**, in the chart on p. 48 and see if any variations apply.

パ The basic form is in column 2, line 6: **ハ** (HA). But to the top-right of the symbol is a small circle, as described in variation 2. (p. 50). This changes the H sound to P. So the reading is PA.

ス Column 4, line 3. No variation. Reading: SU.

So the whole word is PA SU = *pasu* = pass.

Variation 3 Example
Word: **センター**

Find each of the symbols, **セ**, **ン** and **ター**, in the chart on p. 48 and see if variations apply.

セ Column 5, line 3. No variation. Reading: SE

ン Column 7, line 5: Post-vocalic N. No variation. Reading: N

ター The basic form is in Column 2, line 4: タ (TA). But it is followed by a long horizontal stroke. As described in variation 3 (p. 50), this lengthens the vowel. So the TA sound becomes TĀ.

So the whole word is SE N TĀ = *sentā* = centre.

Variation 4 Example
Word: ラック

Find each of the symbols, ラ, ッ, ク, in the chart on p. 48 and see if any variations apply.

ラ Column 2, line 9. No variation. Reading: RA

ッ The basic form is in column 4, line 4: ツ (TSU). But it is smaller than the other symbols in the word. As described in variation 4 (p. 50), this means its function is to indicate a slight pause before the following consonant.

ク Column 4, line 2. Affected by previous ッ. Combined reading: (PAUSE) KU.

So the whole word is RA (PAUSE) KU = *rakku* = ruck.

 Training 15

What are these five rugby positions? Use the chart of basic characters (p. 48) and the list of variations (p. 50 1–4) to find what the words are.

a) フランカー
b) フルバック
c) フライハーフ
d) フッカー
e) プロップ

Time for a break

Sugoi! (Amazing!) You're reading *katakana*! Not long now till you can decipher the whole script! Relax for a minute. Have a cup of tea. (Can you remember how to ask for one?) Or why not count from one to ten...

Ii! (Good!)
Okay, just a little more...

Mō hito'iki!   (One last effort!)

Engage! 16 | *Katakana 3*

In *Engage!* 14 we looked at the basic *katakana* characters and in *Engage!* 15 at four of five variations. Now we'll look at the fifth: combinations of different basic characters in a single syllable.

The possible combinations are shown in the chart opposite. Each combination comprises one of the characters in column 1 followed by one in line 1. As you can see from the table, in combination the first character is full-size and the second character is smaller.

Character combinations in *katakana*

Let's look at a word that includes one of these combinations:

Word: **フィジー**

Look at each of the characters, **フ**, **ィ** and **ジー** .

フ This character is followed by a smaller **ィ** character. This indicates that the two characters are combined in a single syllable.

Try to find this combination in the character combinations chart. **フ** is in column 1, third line from the bottom. Look along the row and find the combination of **フ** and **ィ** in column 3: **フィ**. Reading: FI

ジー The basic form of this character is in column 3, line 3 of the basic character chart (p. 48): **シ** (SHI). But it has two variations.

Firstly, it has two small strokes top-right (variation 1, p. 50). This changes the sound from SHI to JI.

Secondly, it is followed by a long horizontal stroke (variation 3, p. 50). This lengthens the vowel, making the JI sound JĪ.

So the whole word is FI JĪ = *fijī* = Fiji.

That's it! If you made your way through all that, you're now able to read all *katakana* words!

テンサイ *da!* (You're a.........!)

(Try to find how **テンサイ** is read. Then check its meaning from Warm-up 1 on p. 10.)

SECOND CHARACTER (SMALL)								
	ア A	イ I	ウ U	エ E	オ O	ヤ YA	ユ YU	ヨ YO
ウ U		ウィ WI		ウェ WE	ウォ WO			
ヴ VU	ヴァ VA	ヴィ VI		ヴェ VE	ヴォ VO			
キ KI						キャ KYA	キュ KYU	キョ KYO
ギ GI						ギャ GYA	ギュ GYU	ギョ GYO
シ SHI				シェ SHE		シャ SHA	シュ SHU	ショ SHO
ジ JI				ジェ JE		ジャ JA	ジュ JU	ジョ JO
チ CHI				チェ CHE		チャ CHA	チュ CHU	チョ CHO
テ TE		ティ TI					テュ TYU	
デ DE		ディ DI					デュ DYU	
ト TO			トゥ TU					
ド DO			ドゥ DU					
ニ NI						ニャ NYA	ニュ NYU	ニョ NYO
ヒ HI						ヒャ HYA	ヒュ HYU	ヒョ HYO
ビ BI						ビャ BYA	ビュ BYU	ビョ BYO
ピ PI						ピャ PYA	ピュ PYU	ピョ PYO
フ FU	ファ FA	フィ FI		フェ FE	フォ FO			
ミ MI						ミャ MYA	ミュ MYU	ミョ MYO
リ RI						リャ RYA	リュ RYU	リョ RYO

FIRST CHARACTER

To let you display your prowess in deciphering *katakana*, we'll have three summary training sessions: 16 (a) focuses on player names, 16 (b) on team names and 16 (c) on rugby words.

Training 16 (a)

Using the charts and variation list in *Engage!* 14–16, can you identify these record-breaking World Cup players?

a) ジョナ・ロムー　　　　　c) ジョニー・ウィルキンソン

b) ギャビン・ヘイスティングス

(Answers on p. 152)

Training 16 (b)

Which teams (a–d) are in which pools? Write a–d in the correct pools. Refer to the charts and variation list in *Engage!* 14–16.

a) トンガ　　　　　　　c) オーストラリア

b) スコットランド　　　　d) カナダ

Pool A

アイルランド
日本
ロシア
サモア

Pool B

ニュージーランド
イタリア
南(ミナミ)アフリカ
ナミビア

Pool C

イングランド
フランス
アメリカ
アルゼンチン

Pool D

ウェールズ
ジョージア
ウルグアイ
フィジー

(Answers on p. 152)

Training 16 (c)

Match the words with the details in the picture.

a) ゴール
b) タッチライン
c) タッチジャッジ
d) ラインアウト
e) レフェリー
f) ボール

(Answers on p. 152)

Engage! 17 | Venue names in Japanese

Now you've got *katakana* under your belt, let's have a quick look at some more *kanji* (Chinese-style characters). Before you get to Japan why not learn to recognise how the venue names appear in Japanese? First, let's roll out the map and see where things are in alphabet:

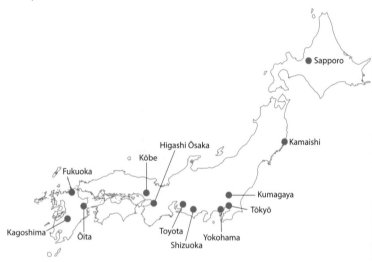

Sapporo

Kamaishi

Higashi Ōsaka

Kōbe

Fukuoka

Kumagaya

Tōkyō

Kagoshima

Ōita

Toyota

Yokohama

Shizuoka

The venue names in *kanji* are shown on the left. The meaning of the *kanji* characters is given on the right.

札幌	*Sapporo*	札 (*satsu* paper money) 幌 (*horo* awning) (This rather odd combination of meanings reflects the fact that the name '*Sapporo*' is not originally Japanese. It comes from the language of the Ainu, the indigenous people of *Hokkaidō* and northern *Honshū*. The *kanji* characters were chosen to represent the pronunciation of the name, rather than to convey any elements of meaning.)
釜石	*Kamaishi*	釜 (*kama* rice pot) 石 (*ishi* stone) (The name *Kamaishi* may also have Ainu origins.)
熊谷	*Kumagaya*	熊 (*kuma* bear) 谷 (*ya* valley)
東京	*Tōkyō*	東 (*tō* east) 京 (*kyō* capital) (*Tōkyō* became the capital city in 1869, replacing the western city of *Kyōto*. *Tōkyō* was previously called *Edo*.)
横浜	*Yokohama*	横 (*yoko* horizontal) 浜 (*hama* beach)
静岡	*Shizuoka*	静 (*shizu* quiet) 岡 (*oka* hill)
豊田	*Toyota*	豊 (*toyo* fruitful) 田 (*ta* rice field) (the character 田 is a graphic image of fields)
大阪	*Ōsaka*	大 (ō big) 阪 (*saka* slope)
神戸	*Kōbe*	神 (*god*) 戸 (*door/house*) With the meaning God's houses, it originally referred to the area around *Ikuta* Shrine (near present-day *Kōbe's Sannomiya* station).
福岡	*Fukuoka*	福 (*fuku* happiness) 岡 (*oka* hill)
熊本	*Kumamoto*	熊 (*kuma* bear) 本 (*moto* source)
大分	*Ōita*	大 (ō big) 分 (bit/cut) ('*ita*' is a unique reading for 分)

Training 17

Try to identify the place names below and draw arrows between them and their positions on the map.

札幌	東京	豊田	福岡
釜石	横浜	大阪	熊本
熊谷	静岡	神戸	大分

That's the end of Part 3

Li zo, ii zo! (Great work!)

Chill-out – The Head Coach's Lecture
Rugby in Japan

Japan's first rugby game was probably played in the 1860s by British soldiers stationed in the newly-established port of *Yokohama*. The sport's introduction at *Keiō* University in 1899 led to increasing popularity among the Japanese themselves, particularly at universities and high schools. The Japan Rugby Football Union was set up in 1926, and a national team was

established for a tour of Canada in 1930. 1932 saw the first test matches on Japanese soil, when a visiting Canadian team was twice beaten by the hosts. The 1930s also saw tours of Japan by teams representing Australian Universities (1934) and New Zealand Universities (1936). The post-war period witnessed the growth of company rugby, with prominent workforce teams from a range of industries competing in the Japan Company Rugby Football Championship. This league was replaced in 2003 by the current Top League. All of the Top League's 16 teams have corporate owners, and many of the players are officially employees of the controlling companies. University rugby remains a very important part of the sport's profile in Japan, with live national TV coverage of the final stages of the University Championship. The final of the High School Championship, dating from 1917, is also broadcast nationally.

Brave Blossoms

The Japanese team's shirts carry an emblem of three cherry blossom flowers. The original rugby shirts of the Japanese team had two open flowers and one bud. The intention was to keep the third bud until Japan played England, that being where the sport originated. In the end, the third blossom appeared when the Japanese team played Oxford University in 1952.

PART 4 | What do we do?

(Essential information for life outside the stadium)

Back in Part 1, you were practising Japanese inside the stadium. A familiar environment – a soothing experience. But how did you get there? And what about food and drink? What about sleep? What about travel? What about etiquette?

These are the types of question we look at in Part 4. You'll find not only practical information and advice but some simple language input too, to make your stay as smooth and enjoyable as possible. You can practise Japanese for visiting a restaurant (see the 'Eat' section, *ENGAGE!* 20), checking in to a hotel ('Sleep' section, *ENGAGE!* 22) and going to a shop ('Shop' section, *ENGAGE!* 23). You'll find important words and phrases for everything from drinking (*ENGAGE!* 21) to emergencies (*ENGAGE!* 26).

The full set of topics ('aims') for the section is on the opposite page, but let's start with a couple of pocket essentials:

> **Mobile phones** – SIM cards for mobile phone use in Japan are available at the main airports. There are internet-only or phone-call-inclusive options. The phone must be unlocked. (You'll find alternative possibilities on-line.)
>
> **Handkerchiefs** – Always carry a handkerchief, as lavatories often do not have hand-drying facilities.

Aims
ENGAGE! 18 – **Transport:** trains, buses, taxis, car rental
ENGAGE! 19 – **Venues and travel:** getting to the venues, what to see nearby, onward connections to other venues and places of interest
ENGAGE! 20 – **Eat:** what types of restaurant there are; where to find them; what to say and what the food is – with help from our illustrated A–Z of Japanese dishes
ENGAGE! 21 – **Drink:** where to get a drink; what the Japanese drinks are; key drinking expressions and etiquette
ENGAGE! 22 – **Sleep:** types of accommodation, what to say, how not to miss breakfast
ENGAGE! 23 – **Shops:** what to expect and key expressions
ENGAGE! 24 – **Etiquette:** behaving well on the street, on the *tatami*…and in the bath
ENGAGE! 25 – **Money:** credit cards, cash, currency exchange and consumption tax
ENGAGE! 26 – **Trouble:** words, phrases and contact points for help with problems and emergencies
ENGAGE! 27 – **Going home:** venue *omiya'ge* – souvenirs Japanese-style

Difficulty: Occasional, light.
Enjoyment rating ○○○○○

This section focuses mainly on trains, although there is also information on buses, taxis and car rental. Air is the easiest way between some venues, but plane journeys are much the same all over the world. Other forms of transport differ from country to country, so a bit of explanation may be helpful.

Before we talk about trains and buses separately a word on passes and smart cards that can be used across different modes of transport.

1. Local day passes

Cities/areas often have day (or multi-day) passes on local transport systems (available from ticket offices) and sometimes there are special discounts for non-Japanese. A *Tōkyō* one-day ticket costs ¥1,590 and can be used on most public transport in the *Tōkyō* area.

2. Smart cards

Smart cards (known as IC cards) are available for use on trains and buses in major cities and surrounding areas, smoothing transfers from one company's services to another's. The names of the cards depend on where you buy them, but all the major ones can be used in different regions. You cannot use them for travel between regions and credit-card registration is required for use for *shinkansen* (bullet) trains, and then only on a limited range of routes. Please note also that IC cards are often not accepted in less populated areas. The card sold by JR (Japan Railways) in the *Tōkyō* region is called *Suica*, and can be purchased from ticket offices, travel service centres and ticket machines. Names of other major cards are *Pasmo*, *Icoca*, *Pitapa*, *Toica*, *Manaca*, *Kitaca*, *Sugoca*, *Nimoca* and *Hayakaken*. IC cards can also be purchased online when you buy a Japan Rail pass (JR pass – see p. 65). Purchase price includes a 500-yen refundable deposit. Topping up the cards is possible at station machines, but requires physical cash. If you have a JR pass, then you would obviously only want to use a smart card on non-JR services.

Trains (*densha*)

On the whole, Japanese trains are wonderful, but they can get very crowded in large cities. Where possible, city rush-hour trains (major cities: 6 or 7–9am; 5 or 6–8pm) should be avoided, particularly if you have luggage. Morning trains are especially busy.

Operators

The main train operator in Japan is JR (Japan Railways), divided up into various regional companies. Many visitors from abroad purchase a **Japan Rail Pass (JR Pass)** which gives 7, 14 or 21 days' travel on the JR group's nationwide services. It can work out as very good value if you travel any long distances (the cost of a 7 day pass is about the same as a return journey between *Tōkyō* and *Kōbe*).

Vouchers for JR passes have to be bought abroad and then exchanged, within 90 days of purchase, at a JR station after you arrive in Japan. This can mean long waits in queues at airport stations.

JR operates the *shinkansen* (bullet trains), other lines between major cities, as well as many local lines, including important services within *Tōkyō*. JR does not run subway services.

There are also a number of other train companies which run their own lines. Most of these lines are relatively short-distance. Prominent companies include *Hankyū*, *Hanshin*, *Kintetsu* and *Nankai* in the *Kansai* region (*Ōsaka/Kōbe/Kyōto*), *Meitetsu* in the *Nagoya* area (including *Toyota*) as well as a number of companies in the *Tōkyō* area, including *Keiō*, *Tōkyū* and *Keisei*.

Ticket sales for JR lines and other lines are normally separate. So without a day pass or IC (Smart) card (p. 64), you will have to buy a new ticket when changing from one company's services to another.

The JR Pass is not valid for journeys on non-JR lines.

Types of service

Shinkansen (新幹線) These (bullet) trains are referred to on announcements as 'super express' trains.

(*Shinkansen* literally means 'new trunk line' and in most cases the trains do not share the lines with other types of train. The stations too are often not shared with older main line services. You will find that many of the *shinkansen* stations have '*shin*' (新) before the place name (e.g. *Shin-Yokohama*). '*Shin*' here, as in *shinkansen*, means 'new' and it is an indication that other services may run through a different, longer-established station in the town. ('*Shin*' in a station name does not always mean it has *shinkansen* services.)

Shinkansen lines have different speeds of service. The following are the categories of train on the main *shinkansen* lines from *Tōkyō* to *Nagoya* and *Ōsaka* and onwards to *Kyūshū*:

- *Nozomi/Mizuho* (stops at largest cities only): JR passes are not valid on these services.

- *Hikari/Sakura* (stops at limited number of stations)

- *Kodama/Tsubame* (stops at all stations)

Generally the best options for JR pass holders on these lines are *Hikari/Sakura* services, with changes onto *Kodama/Tsubame* services when necessary to reach a particular destination.

Be aware that seat reservations are required for some *shinkansen* services that JR pass holders can use. These include the *Hayabusa* services between *Tōkyō* and *Shin-Hakodate-Hokuto* (*Hakodate*) in *Hokkaidō*, and the *Kagayaki* services between *Tōkyō* and *Kanazawa*.

Non-*shinkansen* JR trains have three main speeds of service:

- *Tokkyū* (特急 Limited express): fastest of non-*shinkansen* trains – normally requires a supplement, though not for JR pass holders

- *Kaisoku* (快速 Rapid): more stops than a limited express

- *Futsū* (普通 Local – sometimes called *kaku'eki'teisha* 各駅停車) – these stop at every station

Other operators often use the word *Kyūkō* (急行 Express) for trains slower than *Tokkyū* but faster than *Kaisoku*. Similar trains on JR are referred to as types of *Kaisoku* (Rapid), such as *Tokubetsu-kaisoku* (Special Rapid) or *Shin-kaisoku* (New Rapid).

Types of carriage

The *shinkansen* and many other express trains have the following types of carriage/car:

- Reserved-seat carriages (*shiteiseki* 指定席)
- Non-reserved-seat carriages (*jiyūseki* 自由席)
- Green car (*gurīn-sha* グリーン車) (first class)

There are still some smoking cars on trains, but these are being phased out. Some trains have smoking rooms.

To get a seat reservation you can ask at *midori no madoguchi* (みどりの窓口) ticket offices. Look for the sign shown in the photo. If you have a JR pass, a seat reservation can be obtained for no extra cost.

Train etiquette

- Unless you have a seat reservation, stay in the non-reserved carriage, even if the reserved carriage is empty.
- If you have a seat reservation, only sit in the seat specified.
- Do not put your feet on the seats, unless you take your shoes off first.
- Do not put large items of luggage on the seats.
- Do not talk on mobile phones while sitting in a carriage. Go to the area between the carriages.
- Do not talk loudly.

Queuing

The queues that form on major station platforms can be very confusing, with parallel lines of passengers waiting for different trains from the same platform.

It's difficult to master what's going on. The queue you want will depend on the length of your train, your carriage number and whether your train is first, second or third in order of departure.

But as long as you are on the right platform at the right time, you should be okay.

If in doubt, you can hold out your ticket to somebody in the queue and say:

> **Sumima'sen, kono retsu de ii desu ka?**
> (Excuse me! Is this the right queue?)

Coin lockers コインロッカー *koin rokkā*

Japanese stations normally have lockers of various sizes for passengers' luggage. In some major stations the lockers can be (or in some cases have to be) paid for with an IC (smart) card. In fact it can sometimes be difficult to find a genuine 'coin' locker.

Buses バス *basu*

Ordinary buses are not that easy for foreigners as there is little information in English. You're fine if it's a one-destination bus. Otherwise, it may not be easy to identify the right stop to get off at.

To make it clear where you want to go, say:

> **X ni ikita'i desu.**
> (I want to go to X.)

In urban areas buses accept IC cards, so as long as you have one you just bleep on and off. But in less populated areas IC cards may not be accepted and the payment process can seem complicated. Here it is: unless you're at the bus's starting point, when you get on you'll probably see a ticket (*seiriken* 整理券) waiting for you in the mouth of a machine at the top of the step. Take it. This ticket will carry your stage number. When you want to get off, press the button overhead to alert the driver. Then you pay the amount for your stage number showing on the panel above the windscreen at the front of the bus. The amount has to be inserted into a device beside the driver in exact change. If you don't have exact change, you will be able to obtain it from a change machine beside the driver.

If you don't have a ticket, you will have to pay the full fare from the start of the route. No tickets are issued for passengers who get on at the start of the route.

Taxis タクシー *takushī*

When a taxi is available a sign will be illuminated saying 空車 (*kūsha* – vacant vehicle).

The door will open automatically. Get in and say where you want to go:

> **[Destination name]** *o'nega'i shimasu.*
> [Destination name] please.

On arrival, pay in cash while still seated in the back. No tip is expected. The automatic door will open on the pedestrian (left) side. It will close automatically behind you, so don't slam it shut.

Car rental レンタカー *rentakā*

Car rental can be a good option for less busy areas that are not very well served by trains. Offices are often very conveniently located near stations. Sat Nav is available in English. Make sure the company has an English-language help-line. Reservations can be made on-line or at airports. Prices can be very reasonable. Visitors with licences from most World Cup nations will be able to drive with their national licences plus international driving permits (available in their home countries). French licence holders have to provide translations of their French licences. Holders of licences from Uruguay, Samoa and Tonga may have difficulties hiring vehicles.

Gamba're Map of Japan

RWC locations, key stations and tourist spots

5
6 ● Sapporo
4
2
1
HOKKAIDŌ
7
3
● Hakodate

Aomori
Akita ● Morioka ● **8**
Hanamaki Kamaishi
9
Sado Island
Yamagata
● Niigata **10** ● Sendai
Fukushima
Takasaki
11
2
13
Kumagaya
● Ōmiya
Tōkyō
14
Yokohama

The names of *shinkansen* (bullet train) stations for the following cities on the map have 'Shin' (new) in front of the city name:
    Shin-Aomori
    Shin-Hanamaki
    Shin-Yokohama
    Shin-Ōsaka
    Shin-Kōbe

Hakodate's shinkansen station name is:
    Shin-Hakodate-Hokuto

Rugby venues are shown in red. Circled numbers relate to tourism suggestions mentioned in notes on rugby venues (p.74–108). (No numbers are given for attractions inside towns marked on the map.)

In this section we provide information
on each of the twelve venues in turn,
structured as follows: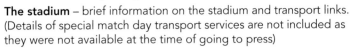

The place – a brief profile of the host
city or region

Getting there – air and train transport
links to the host city or region

The stadium – brief information on the stadium and transport links.
(Details of special match day transport services are not included as
they were not available at the time of going to press)

Places to go nearby – three or four suggestions for tourism in the
area. In choosing them, we tried to think what local people might
recommend.

Further off – other places of interest with reasonable connections
from the host city or region.

Please note:

Train times given are examples. Train times may vary during the
day. Please check online or at a station for actual journey times and
connections at the time of day you wish to travel.

We have chosen the example times with a Japan Rail (JR) pass
holder in mind (see p. 65).

This means:

- The times given do not reflect the *Nozomi* and *Mizuho* services
  on *shinkansen* lines between *Tōkyō* and *Kyūshū*, as JR passes are
  not valid on these services.

- Almost all *shinkansen* journeys between *Tōkyō* (or any other
  station east of *Shin-Ōsaka*) and any station west of *Okayama*
  will involve changing trains at least once (at *Shin-Ōsaka* or
  Okayama). (Only *Nozomi* trains provide a direct through service
  between *Tōkyō* and *Kyūshū* – as far as *Hakata* station, *Fukuoka*.)

- The times given assume that *shinkansen* and express services
  are used where available even for short legs of journeys.
  Please note, that in such cases those without passes may have

reasonably quick alternative routes that avoid the expense of short-distance use of *shinkansen* and other express services.

Unless specified otherwise, all trains mentioned are JR services and can be used without charge by JR pass holders (see p.65).

Where JR uses the term 'Limited Express' (the fastest non-*shinkansen* trains), we normally use the simpler term 'Express'.

Venues

1 *Sapporo* p.74		**7** *Toyota* p.91	
2 *Kamaishi* p.77		**8** *Higashi Ōsaka* p.94	
3 *Kumagaya* p.80		**9** *Kōbe* p.97	
4 *Tōkyō* p.83		**10** *Fukuoka* p.100	
5 *Yokohama* p.86		**11** *Ōita* p.103	
6 *Shizuoka* p.88		**12** *Kumamoto* p.106	

札幌 *Sapporo*

The place

Sapporo (pop. 1.9m) is the largest city in *Hokkaidō*, the northernmost of Japan's four main islands. Inhabited originally only by the Ainu people, significant settlement of *Hokkaidō* by the Japanese dates from the 19th century. Population density is far lower here than in the other main islands and it is known for agriculture, mountains and wilderness. It is home to a number of important national parks. Being in the north, autumn is early and October is usually a good time in *Hokkaidō* for autumn leaves.

Getting there

Air: most visitors will arrive at *Shin-Chitose* Airport (New *Chitose* Airport). Flights include services from *Iwate-Hanamaki*, *Tōkyō (Narita/Haneda)*, *Shizuoka*, *Nagoya (Chūbu* – Centrair), *Ōsaka (Itami/Kankū* – *Kansai* International), *Kōbe* and *Fukuoka*. From the airport to central *Sapporo* takes 37 mins by JR Airport Express.

Train: it is possible to travel to *Sapporo* by train from *Tōkyō*. Take the *Hokkaidō shinkansen* to *Shin-Hakodate-Hokuto* (4 hrs 17 mins) in the south of *Hokkaidō*, and from there an express to *Sapporo* (3 hrs 25 mins). Times between *Shin-Hakodate-Hokuto* and other stations on the *shinkansen* line from *Tōkyō* include: *Shin-Aomori* (1 hr 1 min), *Morioka* (I hr 50 mins), *Sendai* (2 hrs 30 mins) and *Ōmiya* (3 hrs 38 mins). *Hakodate* and other intermediate towns are interesting places to break the journey.

The stadium

The 41,410-capacity *Sapporo* Dome stadium is a 10-min walk from *Fukuzumi* subway station (14 mins from *Sapporo* subway station, which is a 6-min walk from *Sapporo* JR station). The stadium is home to the *Hokkaidō* Nippon-Ham Fighters baseball team and the *Hokkaidō* Consadole *Sapporo* soccer team.

Places to visit nearby

1. Central *Sapporo*

It is interesting to walk around the city centre, taking in *Meiji*-period (1868–1912) buildings, including the Clock Tower, the Old *Hokkaidō* Government Office and *Hokkaidō* University, as well as *Ōdōri Kōen* (park).

2. Historical Village of *Hokkaidō* 北海道開拓の村

18 mins by bus from *Shin-Sapporo* bus terminal (next to *Shin-Sapporo* train station, which is 10 mins by Airport Express train from *Sapporo* station).

A flavour of life in the 19th century when Japanese began to settle in *Hokkaidō* in significant numbers.

3. *Jōzankei Onsen* 定山渓温泉

A hot-spring town one hour's bus ride from *Sapporo*, on the northern edge of the *Shikotsu-Tōya* National Park.

4. *Otaru* 小樽

An attractive old port town 32 mins from *Sapporo* on the JR *Hakodate* line.

Sapporo clock tower

Further off

From *Sapporo* you can reach *Hokkaidō*'s National Parks, though in some cases journey times are long. You can also take the train south to **Hakodate** (attractive historical port town with 19th-century Western buildings) and onwards to *Honshū* (Japan's main island).

Shikotsu-Tōya National Park (south/south-west of *Sapporo*). Lake *Tōya* is accessible from *Sapporo* by JR train to *Tōya* (1 hr 52 mins) and then bus to *Tōyako-onsen* (25 mins), or by direct bus from *Sapporo* (2 hrs 45 mins).

Daisetsuzan National Park (central *Hokkaidō*). One access route is from *Sapporo* to *Asahikawa* JR station (1 hr 30 mins) then bus to *Asahidake-onsen* (1 hr 30 mins).

The following three National Parks in eastern *Hokkaidō* can be accessed by train from *Sapporo* via *Kushiro* (3 hrs 45 mins from *Sapporo* on the fastest Super *Ōzora*). The nearest station for each lies on the *Senmō* line.

Kushiro Wetlands (Kushiro Shitsugen) National Park includes JR *Kushiro Shitsugen* station, 18 mins from *Kushiro*. There are also buses into the park from *Kushiro* station.

Akan Mashū National Park includes the station of *Kawayu-onsen*, 1 hr 30 mins from *Kushiro*.

Shiretoko National Park (north-eastern peninsula – World Heritage) is accessible by bus from JR *Shiretoko-Shari* station, which is 2 hrs 14 mins from *Kushiro*. The bus takes 50 mins to the bus terminal at *Utoro-onsen*, from where, amongst other activities, you can take a cruise up the *Shiretoko* peninsula.

釜石 *Kamaishi*

The place

Kamaishi (pop. 35,000) is on the north-east coast of *Honshū*, the largest of Japan's four main islands. A small coastal city with a strong rugby history, it was devastated by the 2011 *tsunami*. The site of Japan's first Western-style blast furnace, *Kamaishi* was for over a hundred years a major iron/steel production base. *Kamaishi's Nippon* Steel rugby team won both major national rugby tournaments every year 1978–84. *Kamaishi's* current team is called Seawaves.

Getting there

Air: *Iwate-Hanamaki* Airport has flights from *Sapporo* (*Shin-Chitose*), *Nagoya* (*Komaki*), *Ōsaka* (*Itami*) and *Fukuoka*. From *Iwate-Hanamaki* Airport, take a taxi to *Shin-Hanamaki* station for a train to *Kamaishi* (see below). Or there is a bus (7 mins) to JR *Hanamaki Kūkō* (Airport) station, where you can take the *Tōhoku* main line to *Hanamaki* (5 mins) and change for *Kamaishi* (journey time 7–8 mins longer than from *Shin-Hanamaki*).

Train: take the *Tōhokou/Hokkaidō shinkansen* and change at *Shin-Hanamaki* (*Tōkyō* to SH 2hrs 46 mins; SH to *Kamaishi* 1 hr 29 mins by Rapid service – 3 a day, also 7 Local services up to 2 hrs 16 mins). Rapid services also run from *Morioka* (2 hrs 12 mins to *Kamaishi*). *Morioka* is the largest city in *Iwate* prefecture. *Shinkansen* times to *Morioka* include: (from south) *Tōkyō* 2 hrs 11 mins, *Ōmiya* 1 hr 47 mins, *Sendai* 39 mins; (from north) *Shin-Hakodate-Hokuto* in *Hokkaidō*: 1 hr 56 mins; *Shin-Aomori*: 53 mins; *Akita*: 1 hr 43 mins.

The stadium

The newly constructed *Kamaishi* Recovery Memorial Stadium (16,020 capacity) is in *Unosumai*, which is 12 km (15 mins) by bus from *Kamaishi* station.

Places to visit nearby

1. Central *Kamaishi*

A 20-min walk from the station over the river and eastwards across town will take you towards the new wholesale fish market 釜石魚市

場 (*Kamaishi uoichiba*) on the sea-front. Imagine almost everything around you swept away and you will get a sense of the destruction that was caused in 2011. You can walk up a short way to temples on the slopes facing the ocean to get a view over the town. Adjacent to the station is Sun Fish *Kamaishi* (**サン・フィッシュ釜石**) a retail fish market with delicious seafood restaurants. There is a small local museum (**釜石郷土資料館** *Kamaishi kyōdo shiryōkan*) 2 mins from the station (turn right at exit).

2. *Tōno* 遠野

Forty-four mins west of *Kamaishi* by train towards the *shinkansen* stations at *Shin-Hanamaki* and *Morioka*, *Tōno* is a great place to explore by hired bicycle. Surrounded by rice fields, it retains numerous old farm houses and related buildings. A collection of these is found at *Tōno Furusato* Village. (**遠野ふるさと村** *Tōno furusato mura*).

A highly influential folklore collection ('Legends of *Tōno*') was made in the area by *Kunio Yanagita* (1910).

Fields near *Tōno*

3. *Chūson-ji* Temple 中尊寺

Part of the *Hiraizumi* World Heritage site, *Chūson-ji* is a Buddhist temple on a forested hill, dating from 850. Its many National Treasures include the stunning small 12th-century building *Konjiki-dō*. *Hiraizumi* station is approx. 3 hrs from *Kamaishi*, but close to the *shinkansen* line which visitors travel along on the way there and back. From *Kamaishi* take the *Kamaishi* line to *Hanamaki* (1 hr 37 mins). From there you can either take the *Tōhoku* main line direct to *Hiraizumi* (42 mins). Alternatively, you can leave the *Kamaishi* line at *Shin-Hanamaki*, catch a *shinkansen* to *Ichinoseki*, then the *Tōhoku* main line to *Hiraizumi*. Depending on connections, this route can be quicker. The temple is an uphill walk from *Hiraizumi* station. You can hire bicycles to explore more of the *Hiraizumi* site.

Further off

Railways north and south along the coast from *Kamaishi* may still be closed (following the *tsunami* destruction in 2011). So onward train travel normally means making your way back to the *shinkansen* at *Shin-Hanamaki* or *Morioka*, the capital of *Iwate* prefecture.

Morioka is itself a very pleasant city, on the *Kitakami* river with Mt *Iwate* as a backdrop.

From *Morioka* you can easily reach the other *Tōhoku* cities of **Aomori**, **Akita**, and **Sendai**. You can also reach **Hokkaidō** (for journey times see 'Getting there' section, p.77.)

At *Sendai* you can change to the JR *Senzan* line for the mountain temples at **Yamadera** (1 hr). 15 mins further along the *Senzan* line is **Yamagata** city.

熊谷 *Kumagaya*

The place

A city of 200,000 people 60 kilometres north-west of *Tōkyō*. In the *Edo* period (1603–1868), it was a staging post on the *Nakasendō*, one of two main routes between the *shōgun's* power base in *Edo* (current *Tōkyō*) and the then capital, *Kyōto*. The city has a reputation for summer heat and holds the record for the highest temperature ever recorded in Japan: 41.1°C (July 2018).

Getting there

Air: *Narita* and *Haneda* are the most convenient airports for *Kumagaya*. From *Narita* Airport you can take the *Narita* Express to *Tōkyō* station (1 hr) and change for the *Jōetsu* or *Hokuriku shinkansen* to *Kumagaya* (38 mins). Buses are also available (3 hrs).

From *Haneda* Airport (where most domestic flights land) buses take between 2 hrs 15 mins and 3 hrs. Train connections are slightly complicated: *Tōkyō* Monorail (non-JR, but accepts JR passes) to *Hamamatsuchō* (17 mins), change to JR *Yamanote* line for *Tōkyō* station (7 mins), then take the *Jōetsu* or *Hokuriku shinkansen* to *Kumagaya*.

Train: *Kumagaya* is 38 mins by *Jōetsu* or *Hokuriku shinkansen* from *Tōkyō* station. Rail travellers from western Japan (*Tōkaidō*/*Sanyō shinkansen*) should transfer at *Tōkyō*. Travellers coming south on the *Tōhoku*/*Hokkaidō shinkansen* can change at *Ōmiya*, 13 mins south of *Kumagaya*.

The stadium

Kumagaya Rugby Stadium (capacity: 24,000) is 3.5 km (10–15 mins by bus) from the north entrance of *Kumagaya* station.

Places to visit nearby

1. *Menuma Shōdenzan Kangi-in* Temple 妻沼聖天山歓喜院

A temple with remarkable carvings. The main shrine building is a designated National Treasure.

Take a bus from *Kumagaya* station bound for *Ōta*, *Nishi-Koizumi* or *Menuma Shōden-mae*. Get off at *Menuma Shōden-mae* bus stop (23–33 mins).

Menuma Shōdenzan Kangi-in Temple

2. *Nagatoro* River White Water Rafting 長瀞ラインくだり

Thirty-six to fifty-eight mins from *Kumagaya* to *Nagatoro* station on the *Chichibu* Railway (non-JR). Steam locomotive trip available once a day (1 hr 20 mins).

3. *Tomioka* Silk Mill 富岡製糸場

A World Heritage silk mill built in 1872 and initially run by French expatriates. At the time, raw silk was a vital export industry for Japan, and this, the country's first mechanised mill, was twice the size of comparable facilities in Europe. One of the few well-preserved *Meiji* government factory complexes.

From *Kumagaya* take the *Jōetsu shinkansen* to *Takasaki* (15 mins) and change to the *Jōshin* line (non-JR) for *Jōshū Tomioka* station (39 mins). Then a 15-min walk or tourist bus.

4. *Ōmiya Bonsai* Art Museum 大宮盆栽美術館

Bonsai museum and village (a number of *bonsai*-specialist gardens). From *Kumagaya* take the *shinkansen* to *Ōmiya* (13 mins) and change for the *Utsunomiya* line towards *Toro* (3 mins). The museum is a 5-min walk from there.

Further off

Visitors to *Kumagaya* are in easy reach of **Tōkyō**, but they also have opportunities to travel further away from the centre using *shinkansen* connections.

Jōetsu shinkansen trains go on to **Niigata** (1 hr 25 mins) on the Japan Sea coast, with access to **Sado** Island (ferry 2 hrs 30 mins/jetfoil 1 hr 5 mins).

Hokuriku shinkansen trains pass through **Nagano** (*Zenkōji* Temple (7th century); 1998 Winter Olympic host city – 1 hr 10 mins). *Shinkansen* services to the end of the *Hokuriku* line (**Kanazawa** – old streets, *Kenrokuen* garden) do not normally stop at *Kumagaya*. One solution is to take a *shinkansen* in the opposite direction, to *Ōmiya* (13 mins) and change there for *Kanazawa* (2 hrs 9 mins).

From *Ōmiya* you can also catch a *shinkansen* north towards **Sendai**, **Morioka**, **Aomori** and **Hokkaidō** (*Shin-Hakodate-Hokuto*). One reasonably close tourist site in that direction is **Nikkō** (see *Tōkyō* 'Further off' p. 85). From *Ōmiya* take the *Tōhoku shinkansen* to *Utsunomiya* (24 mins) and change for *Nikkō* (*Nikkō* line 49 mins).

東京 *Tōkyō*

The place

Tōkyō has a population of 13.6 million and merges imperceptibly into neighbouring cities in the *Kantō* Plain. The name *Tōkyō* means 'eastern capital' and dates from 1869 when the city replaced *Kyōto* as the capital. Under its former name, *Edo*, it was already the country's largest and most powerful city, having been the *shōgun's* power base since the early 17th century.

Getting there

Air: The *Kantō* region (the area around *Tōkyō* and *Yokohama*) has two major airports: *Narita* and *Haneda*. Japan's leading international airport, *Narita* also has domestic flights from *Fukuoka*, *Sapporo*, *Ōsaka* (*Itami*; *Kankū* – *Kansai* International), *Nagoya* (*Chūbu* – Centrair) and *Ōita*.

From *Narita* Airport the JR *Narita* Express takes you to *Tōkyō* station in 1 hr and *Shinjuku* station in 1 hr 16 mins. Buses also available. (*Shinjuku* is a major station in *Tōkyō*, convenient for trains to the stadium.)

Haneda Airport, also international, is at the same time the country's leading domestic hub. It has flights from *Sapporo*, *Nagoya* (*Chūbu* – Centrair) *Ōsaka* (*Itami*; *Kankū*), *Kōbe*, *Fukuoka*, *Ōita* and *Kumamoto*.

To reach *Tōkyō* from *Haneda* you can take the *Tōkyō* Monorail (non-JR but accepts JR passes) to *Hamamatsuchō* (17 mins). Change to the *Yamanote* line for *Tōkyō* station (7 mins) and *Shinjuku* station (25 mins). Buses also available.

Train: *Tōkyō* is the centre of the country's rail network with *shinkansen* connections with:

1. (*Tōkaidō*/*Sanyō*/*Kyūshū shinkansen*): *Shin-Yokohama* (18 mins); *Nagoya* (1 hr 44 mins), *Kyōto* (2 hrs 40 mins), *Shin-Ōsaka* (2 hrs 53 mins), *Shin-Kōbe* (3 hrs 12 mins), *Hiroshima* (4 hrs 31 mins), *Hakata* (*Fukuoka*) (5 hrs 38 mins), *Kumamoto* (6 hrs 18 mins) and *Kagoshima Chūō* in the south of *Kyūshū* (7 hrs 6 mins).

2. (*Tōhoku*/*Hokkaidō shinkansen*): *Sendai* (1 hr 35 mins), *Morioka* (2 hrs 14 mins), *Shin-Aomori* (3 hrs 21 mins), and *Shin-Hakodate-Hokuto* (4 hrs 17 mins), with onward connections to *Sapporo* (3 hrs 25 mins). Branching off the *Tōhoku shinkansen* line are *shinkansen* routes to *Akita* (3 hrs 49 mins) and *Yamagata* (2 hrs 45 mins).

3. (*Jōetsu/Hokuriku shinkansen*): *Kumagaya* (39 mins), *Niigata* (1 hr 39 mins), *Nagano* (1 hr 25 mins) and *Kanazawa* (2 hrs 32 mins).

The stadium

Tōkyō Stadium (capacity: 49,970) is a 5-min walk from *Tobitakyū* station on the *Keiō* line (non-JR) from *Shinjuku* (23 mins – Special Express to *Chōfu* then change to a Local stopping service). *Shinjuku* station (one of *Tōkyō*'s major terminals) is 13 mins ('Rapid' train) on the JR *Chūō* line from *Tōkyō* station. The stadium is home to soccer teams, FC *Tōkyō* and *Tōkyō* Verdy. It is known more more generally as the *Ajinomoto* Stadium.

Places to visit nearby

The city caters to a huge range of tastes and interests and its pace is often frenetic. The three suggestions we give are ways to find some relative peace and quiet.

1. Take a boat 東京舟めぐり

There are various options, but one idea is to take the boat from *Asakusa* – one of the main tourist areas – to *Hama-rikyū* Garden. Have tea in its *Nakajima no Ochaya* teahouse. From the garden you can walk on to *Shiodome* station on the *Toei Ōedo* subway line (non-JR) (8 mins) or to JR stations at *Shimbashi* (12 mins), and *Hamamatsuchō* (15 mins).

2. *Takahata Fudōson Kongo-ji* Temple 高幡不動尊金剛寺

To the west of *Tōkyō*, an old temple associated with the popular 19th-century hero *Hijikata Toshizō*, who fought for the shogunate against the new *Meiji* government.

A chrysanthemum festival is held from late October to early November. *Takahata Fudō* station is 33 mins on the *Keiō* line Special Express (non-JR) from *Shinjuku*, or 17 mins from *Tobitakyū* (the stadium station), via *Chōfu*.

3. Mount *Takao* 高尾山

A 600-metre mountain to the west of *Tōkyō*. Good exercise to walk to the summit (90 mins). *Takaosan-guchi* station is 47 mins on the (non-JR) *Keiō* line Special Express from *Shinjuku*, or 35 mins from *Tobitakyū* (station for stadium) via *Chōfu*. (You can also take the JR *Chūō* line and change to the (non-JR) *Keiō Takao* line – for *Takaosan-guchi* – at *Takao* station: 45 mins to *Takao* from *Shinjuku*, 60 mins from *Tōkyō* via Special Rapid train.)

Further off

With *Tōkyō* at the centre of the *shinkansen* network, you are well-positioned to make journeys in all directions (see 'Getting there' p. 83), though many major tourist destinations and other large cities are some distance away. One of the closer ones is **Nikkō** (location of huge mountain shrine dedicated to the 17th-century *shōgun Tokugawa Ieyasu*), which can be reached by JR via the *Tōkaidō shinkansen* from *Tōkyō* station to *Utsunomiya* (50 mins), change to *Nikkō* line for *Nikkō* (49 mins). It can also be reached by *Tōbu* Railway (non-JR) direct from *Tōbu Asakusa* station in central *Tōkyō* (1 hr 50 mins; 2 hrs 20 mins). **Nagano** (*Zenkōji* Temple (7th century); 1998 Winter Olympic host city) is in easy reach (1 hr 25 mins from *Tōkyō* station on the *Hokuriku shinkansen*).

Also refer to **Kamakura** and **Lake Ashi** listed under *Yokohama*: 'Places to visit nearby' p. 87.

Kyōto (2 hrs 40 mins) and **Kanazawa** (2 hrs 35 mins) can be given flying visits from *Tōkyō* by *shinkansen*. But if you have time you will probably be better off staying closer by.

Sumida-gawa River, Tōkyō

横浜 *Yokohama*

The place

17 km south west of *Tōkyō*, *Yokohama* is Japan's second-largest city (pop. 3.7 million). A fishing village until the mid-19th century, it became important as a designated international port in 1859, after Japan ended its 200-year policy of national isolation. It is thought to have been in *Yokohama* in 1866 that rugby was first played in Japan.

Getting there

Air: from *Narita* Airport the JR *Narita* Express train reaches *Yokohama* station in 1 hr 35 mins.

From *Haneda* Airport buses reach *Yokohama* in 30–50 mins. By train, take the *Tōkyō* Monorail (non-JR, but accepts JR passes) to *Hamamatsuchō* (17 mins), then the *Keihin Tōhoku* line to *Yokohama* (33 mins). Changing at *Higashi Kanagawa,* can get you to *Shin-Yokohama* (for *shinkansen* and stadium) in 45 mins. *Shin-Yokohama* is 14 mins on the *Yokohama* line from *Yokohama* station. Subway connection 11 mins.

Train: 19 minutes on the *Tōkaidō shinkansen* from *Tōkyō* station to *Shin-Yokohama*. *Tōkaidō/Sanyō/Kyūshū shinkansen* westward connections include: *Nagoya* (1 hr 25 mins), *Kyōtō* (2 hrs 21 mins), *Shin-Ōsaka* (2 hrs 34 mins) *Shin-Kōbe* (2 hrs 53 mins), *Hiroshima* (4 hrs 12 mins), *Hakata* (*Fukuoka*) (5 hrs 19 mins), *Kumamoto* (5 hrs 59 mins), and *Kagoshima Chūō* (6 hrs 47 mins).

The stadium

International Stadium *Yokohama* (capacity 72,327) is 14 mins by foot from *Shin-Yokohama* station. Otherwise known as the *Nissan* Stadium, it is the home of the soccer team, *Yokohama* F Marinos.

Places to visit nearby

1. *Sankeien* Garden 三渓園

A large and renowned Japanese garden 35 mins by bus from *Yokohama* station (East Entrance, Bus 8 or 148. Get off at *Sankeien-iriguchi*.) *Yokohama* station is 14 mins on the *Yokohama* line from *Shin-Yokohama* station. Subway connection 11 mins.

2. *Great Buddha* at *Kōtoku-in* Temple, *Kamakura*
鎌倉大仏殿高徳院

Kamakura is 30 mins by JR *Yokosuka* line from *Yokohama* station.
A town with wonderful temples, including *Kōtoku-in* with its giant
statue of the Buddha.

3. Lake *Ashi* (*Ashinoko*) 芦ノ湖

One of five major lakes near Mount *Fuji*, within the long-established
mountain resort area of *Hakone*. From *Shin-Yokohama* take the
shinkansen to *Odawara* (16 mins) and change to the *Odakyū* line
(non-JR). At *Hakone Yumoto* change to *Hakone Tozan* mountain
railway (non-JR) to *Gōra* (59 mins from *Odawara*). Then you can
take a cable car (10 mins) and finally a ropeway (30 mins) to the
shores of Lake *Ashi*.

Further off

Being under 20 mins south of *Tōkyō*, your situation is not much
different to being in *Tōkyō*, though slightly further from cities in the
north and slightly closer to cities in the west. The difference reduces
the *shinkansen* time to **Kyōto** (2 hrs 21 mins), for example, making
a day trip a little easier.

Giant Buddha, *Kamakura*

静岡県 *Shizuoka*

The place

Shizuoka prefecture lies between *Tōkyō/Yokohama* to the east and *Nagoya*, *Kyōto* and *Ōsaka* to the west. Traditionally a major tea-growing area, its well-known industries now include *Suzuki* motors, *Yamaha* motorcycles and pianos, and *Honda* transmissions. The eastern end of the prefecture includes the southern slopes of Mount *Fuji* – visible to the right of the train if travelling from *Tōkyō/Yokohama*. (NB: the Mt *Fuji* climbing season lasts from early July to early September.) The *Shizuoka* stadium is at *Aino*, in the small city of *Fukuroi* (pop. 80,000) whose industries include tea, melons and *Yamaha* outboard motors. In the *Edo* period (1603–1868) *Fukuroi* was the central point on the *Tōkaidō* road, one of two routes from the *shōgun*'s power base in *Edo* (today's *Tōkyō*) to the former capital, *Kyōto*. The location is marked by a small tea-house evocative of *Hiroshige*'s print from his Fifty-three Stations of the *Tōkaidō* (p. 90).

Getting there

Air: From *Narita* Airport you can take the *Narita* Express to *Tōkyō* station for *shinkansen* connections (see Train below). From *Haneda* Airport the *shinkansen* can be reached by bus to *Shin-Yokohama* station. *Chūbu* (Centrair) Airport (*Nagoya*) is another major airport convenient for *Shizuoka*.

The nearest airport to the stadium is *Mt Fuji Shizuoka*, with flights from *Sapporo* (*Shin-Chitose*) and *Fukuoka*. *Mt Fuji Shizuoka* Airport is 48 mins by bus from *Shizuoka* station or 25 mins to *Shimada* station for a JR train to *Aino* (23 mins).

Train: the *Tōkaidō shinkansen* runs through the prefecture, with stops including *Shizuoka* city, *Kakegawa* and *Hamamatsu*. These last two are the best places to change from the *shinkansen* to the *Tōkaidō* main line to reach the stadium at *Aino*. Fastest journey times (journeys involve train changes) to *Aino* include (eastwards) *Shin-Yokohama* (1 hr 31 mins), *Tōkyō* (1 hr 50 mins), and (westwards) *Nagoya* (57 mins), *Kyōto* (1 hr 35 mins), *Shin-Ōsaka* (1 hr 50 mins), *Shin-Kōbe* (2 hrs 4 mins), *Hiroshima* (3 hrs 24 mins), and *Hakata* (*Fukuoka*) (4 hrs 23 mins).

The stadium

The 50,889-capacity *Shizuoka* Stadium Ecopa is in *Fukuroi* city, near *Aino* station on the *Tōkaidō* main line, between *Fukuroi* (3 mins) and *Kakegawa* (6 mins), which is on the *shinkansen* line. The nearest bigger cities are *Hamamatsu* (20 mins *Tōkaidō* main line) and *Shizuoka* (14 mins from *Kakegawa* on the *shinkansen*). The stadium is walking distance (15 mins) from *Aino* station.

Places to visit nearby

1. *Yusan-ji* Temple 油山寺

A Buddhist temple in a wooded setting 15 mins by taxi from *Fukuroi* station. Founded in 701. Its waterfall is said to have restored the eyesight of the 8th-century Empress *Kōken*.

2. *Miho no Matsubara* 三保の松原

Part of the World Heritage Mount *Fuji* cultural site, *Miho no Matsubara* is a pine-tree lined stretch of coastline with a view of Mount *Fuji*. It is the scene of the story of *Hagoromo*, on which a famous *Nō* drama is based. In early October, a *Hagoromo* Festival is held here with a night-time outdoor performance of the play.

From *Kakegawa* (6 mins on the *Tōkaidō* main line from *Aino*) take the *shinkansen* to *Shizuoka* (14 mins) and change to the *Tōkaidō* main line for *Shimizu* (11 mins). From there you can reach *Miho no Matsubara* by a 15-min boat ride from *Shimizu* Harbour, easily accessible from the station. Or you can take a *Miho-Yamanote*-line bus to *Miho-no-Matsubara-iriguchi* (25 mins), from where you have a 20-min walk.

3. *Ōigawa* Steam Railway/*Yume no Tsuribashi* (Bridge of Dreams) Suspension Bridge 大井川鉄道/夢の吊橋

Take the *Tōkaidō* main line from *Aino* to *Kanaya* (18 mins). Change to the *Ōigawa* Railway main line (non-JR), get off at the next station (*Shin-Kanaya*) for the steam train to *Senzu*. The steam trains run three times a day in each direction (1 hr 15 mins).

To visit the long pedestrian suspension bridge (*Yume no Tsuribashi*) across the *Sumatakyō* Gorge, take a bus from *Senzu* to *Sumatakyō-iriguchi* (39 mins), a short distance from *Sumatakyō-onsen*.

Further off

Convenient for the major cities of both east and west Japan, including the old capital **Kyōto**, *Shizuoka* prefecture can be a good base. If you have a JR pass, you can travel at will in either direction.

Remaining within *Shizuoka* prefecture, you could travel to the **Izu** Peninsula. One attraction is boat rides at *Dōgashima* on the west coast of the peninsula: (**Dōgashima Cave Cruise 堂ヶ島洞窟めぐり**). From *Kakegawa* (6 mins on the *Tokaidō* line from *Aino*) take the *shinkansen* to *Mishima* (46 mins), change to the *Izu-Hakone* Railway *Sunzu* line (non-JR) for *Shuzenji* (40 mins), a pleasant hot-spring town. Then take a bus (90 mins) to *Dōgashima*.

To visit **Lake Ashi** (see *Yokohama*: 'Places to visit nearby' – p. 87) take the *shinkansen* to *Odawara* (1 hr 1 min from *Kakegawa*).

Tea Stall at *Fukuroi* by *Utagawa Hiroshige*
(Fifty-three Stations of the *Tōkaidō*)

豊田 *Toyota*

The place

Toyota City (pop. 420,000) in *Aichi* prefecture is between *Tōkyō/ Yokohama* to the east and *Kyōto/Ōsaka* to the west. Home of *Toyota* Motor Corporation, it is part of Japan's third-largest metropolitan area, centred on *Nagoya* (25 km north-west of *Toyota*).

Getting there

Air: *Nagoya* (*Komaki*) Airport (with flights from *Iwate-Hanamaki*, *Fukuoka* and *Kumamoto*) is 30 mins by bus from *Nagoya* JR station.

The larger (international) *Chūbu* Airport (Centrair) has flights from *Sapporo* (*Shin-Chitose*), *Tōkyō* (*Haneda*), *Fukuoka*, *Kumamoto* and *Ōita*. *Chūbu* Airport is 28 mins by *Meitetsu* Railway Airport Express (non-JR) from *Meitetsu Nagoya* station. There are bus services from the airport to *Toyota* (1 hr 25 mins).

Train: the closest major *shinkansen* station to *Toyota* is *Nagoya*. *Toyohashi* further east is another possible transfer point.

The *shinkansen* links *Nagoya* with *Shin-Yokohama* (1 hr 25 mins) and *Tōkyō* (1 hr 44 mins) to the east, and, to the west, *Kyōto* (37 mins), *Shin-Ōsaka* (51 mins), *Shin-Kōbe* (1 hr 6 mins), *Hiroshima* (2 hrs 25 mins), *Hakata* (*Fukuoka*) (3 hrs 32 mins) *Kumamoto* (4 hrs 12 mins) and *Kagoshima Chūō* (5 hrs).

To reach *Toyota* from *Nagoya*, take the *Meitetsu* Railway (non-JR) from *Meitetsu Nagoya* station to *Toyota-shi* (58 mins). *Meitetsu Nagoya* station is just to the east of *Nagoya* JR station.

From *Toyohashi*, transfer to the *Tōkaidō* main line as far as *Okazaki* (20 mins). Then take the *Aichi* Loop line (non-JR) to *Shin-Toyota* (30 mins).

The stadium

The City of *Toyota* Stadium (capacity: 45,000) is the base of the *Nagoya* Grampus Football Club (founded by *Toyota* Motor Corp.), as well of *Toyota* Verblitz (the *Toyota*-owned rugby club). It is a 15-min walk from *Toyota-shi* station or 17-min walk from *Shin-Toyota* station.

Places to visit nearby

1. *Toyota Kaikan* Museum トヨタ会館

Museum at *Toyota* Motor Corp. factory. Plant tours available if booked in advance. A 25-min *Meitetsu* bus ride from *Toyota-shi* station. See *Toyota Kaikan* website for other possible routes.

2. *Inuyama* Castle 犬山城

One of Japan's oldest castles, and one of only five designated as National Treasures. Approach the castle along the riverside from *Inuyama-yūen* station (10-min walk), or through the town (15–20 min walk) from *Inuyama* station, including an old street leading up to the castle. (Or you could go one way there, the other way back.) Near the castle is the beautiful *Uraku-en* Garden, with a 17th-century National Treasure tea hut. You can have traditional Japanese tea in another building in the grounds. 1 hr 18 mins on the *Meitetsu* Railway network (non-JR) from *Toyota-shi* to *Inuyama* (26 mins from *Meitetsu Nagoya*). *Inuyama-yūen* is 2 mins further on. The nearest JR station is *Unuma* (20-min walk to the castle). Reaching *Unuma* from JR *Nagoya* normally involves a change of trains at *Gifu*.

Inuyama Castle

3. *Meiji-mura* 明治村

A collection of some 60 buildings from the *Meiji* Period (1868–1912) brought together from different parts of Japan and beyond. Takes I hr 18 mins on the *Meitetsu* Railway network (non-JR) from *Toyota-shi* to *Inuyama* (26 mins from *Meitetsu Nagoya*). Then a 20-min bus ride. If you have a whole day, combining *Meiji-mura* and *Inuyama* Castle (above) may be an option.

Further off

The *Nagoya/Aichi* area is conveniently situated for visiting both east and west Japan. The old capital **Kyōto**, in particular is just 38 mins away from *Nagoya* by *shinkansen*.

Nagoya also has good non-*shinkansen* connections. Destinations include: the **Japan Alps** region – **Takayama** (old streets; *Jinya* – unique *Edo* period govt building; festivals – autumn festival 9th–10th Oct.) (2 hrs 13 mins), **Hida Furukawa** (small traditional town) (2 hrs 32 mins) and **Matsumoto** (castle) (2 hrs 4 mins). The line to *Matsumoto* passes through *Nakatsugawa* (50 mins), from where you can catch a bus (35 mins) to **Magome** to walk part of the old **Nakasendō** road. It also passes through *Tajimi*, home to the 14th-century *Kokeizan Eihōji* Temple, with two buildings classified as National Treasures. Beyond *Matsumoto* lies **Nagano** (2 hrs 59 mins – 7th-century *Zenkōji* temple; 1998 Winter Olympic host city). The major historical town **Kanazawa** (*samurai* streets; *Kenrokuen* garden) can also be reached from *Nagoya* (2 hrs 58 mins direct/2 hrs 30 mins via *Maibara* (which is on the *shinkansen* line west of *Nagoya*). There are buses from *Takayama* and *Kanazawa* to **Shirakawa-gō** (World Heritage area of long-roof thatched farmhouses).The *Nanki* express train runs from Nagoya three times a day down the coast of the *Kii* Peninsula to **Kii Katsuura** (3 hrs 51 mins), Japan's leading tuna port, from where you can access the World Heritage **Kumano Kodō** pilgrim route (also accessible from *Ōsaka*, see p. 96.) Although a JR train, pass-holders pay a supplement on the *Nanki* service because of partial track sharing.)

東大阪 *Higashi Ōsaka*

The place

The city of *Higashi* (East) *Ōsaka* (pop. 500,000) borders *Ōsaka* city, the centre of western Japan's major commercial and industrial area. *Higashi Ōsaka* came into being in 1967 with the amalgamation of three towns. The surrounding region is known as *Kansai*, which includes not only *Ōsaka*, but *Kōbe*, *Kyōto* and neighbouring prefectures.

Getting there

Air: *Kansai* International Airport (*Kankū*), the region's international hub, is 50 mins by JR *Haruka* express train to *Shin-Ōsaka* station or, for the stadium vicinity, take the airport bus to *Kintetsu Uehonmachi* station for a *Kintetsu Nara* line train (non-JR) to *Higashi Hanazono* (1 hr 10 mins in total).

Kankū has domestic flights from *Sapporo* (*Shin-Chitose*), *Tōkyō* (*Narita*; *Haneda*), *Fukuoka* and *Kumamoto*.

Itami Airport is 29 mins by train from central *Ōsaka*. Take the Monorail (non-JR) to *Hotarugaike* station and change to the *Hankyū Takarazuka* line (non-JR) for *Hankyū Umeda* station (adjacent to JR *Ōsaka*. *Itami* has flights from *Sapporo* (*Shin-Chitose*), *Iwate-Hanamaki*, *Tōkyō* (*Narita*; *Haneda*), *Fukuoka*, *Ōita* and *Kumamoto*.

Train: the nearest *shinkansen* station is *Shin-Ōsaka*. Times between *Shin-Ōsaka* and other major *shinkansen* stations include (to the east) *Kyōto* (15 mins), *Nagoya* (51 mins), *Shin-Yokohama* (2 hrs 35 mins) and *Tōkyō* (2 hrs 54 mins), and (to the west) *Shin-Kōbe* (13 mins), *Hiroshima* (1 hr 26 mins), *Hakata* (2 hrs 33 mins), *Kumamoto* (3 hrs 13 mins), and *Kagoshima Chūō* (4 hrs 1 min). *Shin-Ōsaka* station is 4 mins by JR from *Ōsaka* station.

The stadium

The 24,100-capacity *Hanazono* Rugby Stadium is a 14-min walk from *Higashi Hanazono* station on the *Kintetsu Nara* line (non-JR).

To reach *Higashi Hanazono* from *Shin-Ōsaka* take the *Kōbe* line from *Shin-Ōsaka* to *Ōsaka*, then the JR Loop line to *Tsuruhashi*, where you change to the *Kintetsu Nara* line (non-JR) for *Higashi Hanazono* (total journey time: 40–60 mins). You can also take an

Ōsaka Metro *Midōsuji* line (non-JR) to *Namba* station and change to the *Kintetsu Nara* line (non-JR) running from the adjacent *Ōsaka Namba* station (42 mins). Although theoretically quicker, without a guide to help you this second choice is probably more confusing.

Constructed in 1929, *Hanazono* is the oldest dedicated rugby stadium in Japan. It is currently home to the *Kintetsu* Liners rugby team.

Places to visit nearby

1. *Ishikiri Tsurugiya* Shrine 石切劔箭神社

A prominent *Shintō* shrine, a 12-min walk from *Ishikiri* station, four stops (8 mins) from *Higashi Hanazono* on the *Kintetsu Nara* line. Also accessible from *Shin-Ishikiri* station (7-min walk) on the *Kintetsu Keihanna* Line (28 mins from *Ōsaka* Metro *Higashi Umeda* station, which is adjacent to *Ōsaka* JR station).

2. *Kuromon* Market 黒門市場

Fish and general market. Exit 10 from *Nippombashi* station on the *Ōsaka* Metro *Sennichimae* line (non-JR).

3. Open-air Museum of Old Japanese Farmhouses 日本民家集落博物館

1km on foot from *Ryokuchi-kōen* station on the *Kita Ōsaka Kyūkō* line (non-JR) – 7 mins from *Shin-Ōsaka*.)

Dōtombori district of *Osaka*

Further off

The Ōsaka area is extremely convenient for visiting the former capital **Kyōto**, just 15 mins east from *Shin-Ōsaka* station by *shinkansen*. To the west beyond *Kōbe* some *shinkansen* trains stop at **Himeji** (44 mins from *Shin-Ōsaka*), site of the World Heritage **Himeji Castle** (see *Kōbe*: 'Places to visit nearby' p.98). Also to the west lies **Okayama** and **Hiroshima**, 52 mins and 1 hr 32 mins from *Shin-Ōsaka* respectively. See *Kōbe*: 'Further off' p.99.

Non-*shinkansen* destinations include: the World Heritage sites of the ancient capital **Nara**, which is 32 mins from *Higashi Hanazono* (the stadium station) on the *Kintetsu Nara* line (non-JR). By JR it is 54 mins from *Ōsaka* station on the *Kansai* main line. The World Heritage temple of **Hōryūji** is also on the *Kansai* main line, three stops (12 mins) closer to *Ōsaka*. *Nankai Namba* station (non-JR) gives access to **Mt. Kōya** (World Heritage hill-top Buddhist temples dating from 815) (1 hr 32 mins to *Gokurakubashi* station). **Kumano Kodō**, (ancient World Heritage pilgrim route) is accessible by JR *Kuroshio* express from *Shin-Ōsaka* (2 hrs 16 mins to *Kii Tanabe*; 4 hrs to **Kii Katsuura** – also accessible from *Nagoya*: see *Toyota* 'Further off' p.93).

神戸 Kōbe

The place

Like *Yokohama*, *Kōbe* was one of the first ports to be opened to foreign trade after the abandonment of Japan's two-century isolationist policy in the 1850s. Just 28 km west of *Ōsaka*, *Kōbe* is now Japan's seventh-largest city (pop. 1.5 million). The city suffered a major earthquake in 1995.

Getting there

Air: *Kōbe* Airport has flights from *Tōkyō* (*Haneda*) and *Sapporo* (*Shin-Chitose*). The non-JR Port Liner service takes 18 mins to get to *Sannomiya* station, close to *Shin-Kōbe* shinkansen station. Other nearby airports: *Kankū* (*Kansai* International, the region's international hub) and *Itami* (*Ōsaka*), from which buses to *Kōbe* take 65 mins and 40 mins respectively.

Train: *Shinkansen* services arrive at *Shin-Kōbe* station. Journey times include: (to the east – journeys beyond *Shin-Ōsaka* may involve train changes) *Shin-Ōsaka* (13 mins), *Kyōto* (29 mins), *Nagoya* (1 hr 5 mins), *Shin-Yokohama* (2 hrs 53 mins) and *Tōkyō* (3hrs 11 mins), and (to the west) *Hiroshima* (1 hr 12 mins), *Hakata* (*Fukuoka*) (2 hrs 19 mins), *Kumamoto* (2 hrs 59 mins) and *Kagoshima Chūō* (3 hrs 47 mins).

The stadium

The nearest station to the 30,132-capacity *Kōbe Misaki* Stadium (Noevir) is *Misaki Kōen* on the (non-JR) *Kōbe* Subway *Kaigan* line, 25 mins (change at *Shin-Nagata*) from *Shin-Kōbe* (*shinkansen*) station. Or take the *Seishin Yamate* subway line to *Sannomiya* and walk to *Hanadokei-mae* on the *Kaigan* line for a train to *Misaki Kōen* (23 mins in total including 8-min walk). The stadium is the home of the *Kōbe* Steel Rugby Club (Kobelco Steelers), as well as of Vissel *Kōbe* FC.

Places to visit nearby

1. **Within walking distance of *Shin-Kōbe* station:**
   a. ***Kōbe Kitano Ijinkan-gai* 神戸北野異人館街**
      An area of Western-style houses lived in by Europeans and

Americans during the *Meiji* period (1868–1912). A 15-min walk from either *Shin-Kōbe* or *Sannomiya* stations. Buildings that can be visited include the *Moegi* (light green) house and the *Kazamidori* (weathercock) house. One interesting route is a forested path to the north of *Shin-Kōbe* station. This can be combined with a visit to the *Nunobiki* Falls (see below).

b. *Nunobiki Falls*. 布引の滝

A 15–20-min uphill walk directly from *Shin-Kōbe* station leads to one of Japan's 'three great divine waterfalls'. Good view across the city.

2. *Hakutsuru Sake* Brewery Museum 白鶴酒造資料館

A former *sake* brewery building displaying traditional brewing methods. Next to the present-day *Hakutsuru* Brewery. *Hakutsuru* means 'white crane'.

Sumiyoshi station on the *Hanshin* (non-JR) main line (11 mins from *Sannomiya* in central *Kōbe*, plus 5-min walk.)

3. *Himeji* Castle 姫路城

World Heritage castle built in 1609. The striking white building is often compared to a bird taking flight and is sometimes called the 'heron' or 'egret' castle, contrasting with the black 'crow' castle of *Matsumoto*. *Shinkansen* to *Himeji* from *Shin-Kōbe* station (26 mins), then a 20-min walk, or a bus from *Himeji* station.

Weathercock House, *Kōbe*

Further off

(See also suggestions for *Higashi Ōsaka* (p. 96), *Shin-Ōsaka* being just 13 mins from *Shin-Kōbe* by *shinkansen*.)

Kōbe is convenient for visits by *shinkansen* westward to **Okayama** (32 mins – *Kōrakuen* garden), **Onomichi** (steeply hilled port, film location – 1 hr 19 mins change for *Sanyō* main line at *Fukuyama*), **Hiroshima** (1 hr 14 mins) and **Miyajima** island (26 mins from *Hiroshima* on *Sanyō* main line plus 10-min ferry). NB: The iconic *torii* gate is due to be undergoing renovation during the World Cup. From *Onomichi* you can reach **Shikoku** by hired bicycle (80 km *Shimanami Kaidō*) – for train and bus routes to Shikoku, see below.

Links from *Okayama* include: **Kurashiki** (old streets – 15 mins *Sanyō* main line) and **Naoshima** (art island – 50-min train to *Uno* – *Uno* line, normally changing at *Chayamachi* – then 20-min ferry).

Okayama also has trains south to *Shikoku* – times to major cities are: **Takamatsu** 54 mins (*Ritsurin Kōen* – 17th-century garden), **Matsuyama** 2 hrs 40 mins by *Shiokaze* express (*Dōgo Onsen*, old hot spring bath-house); **Kōchi** 2 hrs 34 mins by *Nampū* express, passing near **Iya** valley at **Ōboke** (1 hr 36 mins – river gorge boat trips).

Northward, the *Yakumo* express links *Okayama* to **Matsue** (2 hrs 36 mins), from where **Izumo Taisha** (Grand Shrine) is reached in about an hour (non-JR *Ichibata* line from *Matsue Shinjiko Onsen* station or JR to *Izumo-shi*, change to *Ichibata* line to *Izumo Taisha-mae*).

Shikoku is also reached by bus (reservations recommended) from *Shin-Kōbe* or *Sannomiya* over *Awaji* island to **Naruto**. The same bus runs near *Maiko* JR station (27 mins from *Shin-Kōbe* – *shinkansen* to *Nishi Akashi*, change for *Sanyō* main line to *Maiko*, 5-min walk plus elevator to bus stop. NB: route to the elevator is not obvious). Between *Awaji* island and *Shikoku* is one of the world's most powerful whirlpools (alight bus at *Naruto Kōen-guchi* – 1 hr 48 mins from *Shin-Kōbe*). View by boat, or glass-bottomed walkway. Check *Naruto* Straits tide information on-line for best visit times. Also near *Naruto* is the start of *Shikoku*'s 88-temple pilgrimage (*Ryōzen-ji* temple, a short walk from *Bandō* station – 23 mins from *Naruto* station, change at *Ikenotani*). *Bandō* also has a former WW1 POW camp and museum (*Naruto* German House – the prisoners were German, captured in Tsingtao, China).

福岡 Fukuoka

The place

Fukuoka (pop. 1.5 million) is the largest city in *Kyūshū*, the southern- and westernmost of Japan's four main islands. In the north of the island, with *Kita-kyūshū* city, it forms one of Japan's most important industrial areas. The name of the station, *Hakata*, is that of a town which merged with *Fukuoka* in 1876.

Getting there

Air: *Fukuoka* Airport is 5 mins by (non-JR) subway (*Kūkō* line) from *Hakata* station. It has flights from *Sapporo* (*Shin-Chitose*), *Iwate-Hanamaki*, *Tōkyō* (*Narita*; *Haneda*), *Nagoya* (*Komaki*; *Chūbu* – Centrair) and *Ōsaka* (*Itami*; *Kankū* – *Kansai* International).

Train: *Fukuoka's Hakata* station has *shinkansen* connections (east) with *Hiroshima* (1 hr 6 mins), *Shin-Kōbe* (2 hrs 20 mins), *Shin-Ōsaka* (2 hrs 33 mins), *Kyōto* (3 hrs 17 mins), *Shin-Yokohama* (5 hrs 36 mins) and *Tōkyō* (5 hrs 55 mins), and (south) with *Kumamoto* (40 mins) and *Kagoshima Chūō* (1 hr 28 mins).

Travelling from *Ōita*, take the direct Sonic Express to *Hakata* (2 hrs 2 mins), or the JR *Nippō* line north to *Kokura* (1hr 20 mins) and change to the west-bound *shinkansen* for *Hakata* (16 mins).

The stadium

Fukuoka Hakatanomori Stadium (capacity 20,049) is 20–30 mins by bus from *Hakata* station. *Fukuoka* Airport station is a starting point for buses to the stadium on normal domestic match days though there is no regular daily service. The stadium's other name is Level5 Stadium, and it is is the home ground of Avispa *Fukuoka* FC.

Places to visit near by

1. *Nokonoshima* Island 能古島

Take the *Fukuoka* subway *Kūkō* line (non-JR) to *Meinohama* station (19 mins), then a bus to the ferry terminal (15 mins), or take a direct bus from *Hakata* station (42 mins). The crossing takes 10 mins. The Island Park is normally bright with cosmos flowers in September and October.

2. *TŌTŌ* Museum TOTO ミュージアム

Leading Japanese sanitaryware manufacturer displays its 102 years of lavatories and latest small-room technology. Not standard sightseeing, but perhaps interesting to visit a bit of corporate Japan. *Shinkansen* to *Kokura* then *Nippō* line to *Minami Kokura* (33 mins total). Then a 10-min walk.

3. *Dazaifu Tenmangū* Shrine 太宰府天満宮

A shrine built over the grave of 9th-century scholar *Sugawara no Michizane.* By his posthumous name *Tenjin*, he is revered around Japan as a god of literature and learning. Students visit the shrine in hope of exam success. *Nishitetsu* line (non-JR) from *Nishitetsu Fukuoka (Tenjin)* to *Futsukaichi*, then change for *Dazaifu* (28 mins) plus 5-min walk.

Dazaifu Tenmangū Shrine

Further off

As the largest city in *Kyūshū*, *Fukuoka* has advantages as a starting point for travel in that region. It is worth noting that it is also little more than an hour by *shinkansen* from **Hiroshima** (on *Honshū*.)

A major destination in *Kyūshū* is **Nagasaki** to the south-west of *Fukuoka* (2 hrs by *Nagasaki* main line express from *Hakata* station). The same line can be used on trips to **Shimabara** (*samurai* houses, street waterways) (3 hrs 3 mins) – change at *Isahaya* (1 hr 37 mins) for the non-JR *Shimabara* Railway line.

Shimabara and *Nagasaki* have bus services to *Unzen* village in the **Unzen-Amakusa** National Park (see *Kumamoto*: 'Further off' p. 108).

Nagasaki also gives access to *Gunkanjima* (Battleship Island), real name **Hashima**, a Japanese Industrial Revolution World Heritage site that features in the James Bond film *Skyfall*. The island's history includes use of forced Chinese and Korean labour in the 1930s and '40s.

Hirado, like *Nagasaki*, a major early trading port with the West, can be reached from *Hakata* station in 3 hrs 15 mins, changing at **Arita** (pottery town – 1 hr 23 mins)) for the *Matsuura* Railway *Nishi Kyūshū line* (non-JR). The line passes through **Imari** (pottery town – 23 mins from *Arita*). *Karatsu* (pottery town) can be reached in 49 mins from *Imari* (JR *Chikuhi* line). To reach *Karatsu* from *Fukuoka* city, take the non-JR *Kūkō* subway line as far as *Meinohama*. From there the line continues as JR line to *Karatsu* (1 hr 18 mins from *Hakata* station).

The *shinkansen* line gives easy access to **Kumamoto** (39 mins – see p. 106) and **Kagoshima** (1 hr 30 mins) in the south of *Kyūshū* (see *Kumamoto*: 'Further off', p. 107).

大分 Ōita

The place

Ōita city is the capital and largest city (pop. 480,000) of *Ōita* prefecture on the eastern side of *Kyūshū*. In the 15th and 16th centuries it was a leading port for trade with China and Portugal, and the surrounding area was one in which Jesuit missionaries had considerable success. Francis Xavier visited in 1551, welcomed by *Ōtomo Sōrin* a prominent lord (*daimyō*) who converted to Christianity. *Sōrin*'s statue stands outside the station. The large hot-spring resort town of *Beppu* is 8 mins north by train, with a number of big hotels.

Getting there

Air: *Ōita* Airport is 60 mins by bus from JR *Ōita* station. The airport has flights from the *Tōkyō* area (*Narita*; *Haneda*), *Nagoya* (*Chūbu* – Centrair) and *Ōsaka* (*Itami*). Alternative airport: *Fukuoka* (see *Fukuoka* section p. 100).

Train: Take the *Sanyō/Kyūshū shinkansen* to *Kokura* and change for the 1-hr-20-min *Nippō* line ride to *Ōita*. *Shinkansen* times between *Kokura* and other cities include: *Tōkyō*: 5 hrs 38 mins; *Shin-Yokohama*: 5 hrs 19 mins; *Nagoya*: 3hrs 53 mins, *Kyōto*: 3 hrs; *Shin-Ōsaka*: 2 hrs 16 mins; *Shin-Kōbe*: 2 hrs 3 mins; *Hiroshima*: 50 mins; *Hakata* (*Fukuoka*): 16 mins; *Kumamoto*: 56 mins.

The stadium

Ōita Stadium (capacity 40,000) is 35 mins by bus from *Ōita* station. Otherwise known as *Ōita* Bank Dome or Big Eye, it is the home of *Ōita* Trinita FC.

Places to visit nearby

1. Mt *Takasaki* Wild Japanese Monkey Park 高崎山自然動物公園

25-min *Ōita Kōtsū* bus ride from *Ōita* station. Board a bus heading for *Sekinoe*, *Kannawa*, or *Kunisaki*. Get off at the *Takasakiyama Shizen Dōbutsuen-mae* bus stop. The park includes a 628-metre mountain where the monkeys live wild. Next door is an aquarium with dolphins.

2. *Usuki* Stone Buddha Statues 臼杵石仏

National Treasure stone Buddha carvings thought to date from the 12th century. *Usuki* was where the shipwrecked English sailor William Adams (featured in James Clavelll's 'Shogun') reached land in 1600. He became an advisor to the first *Tokugawa shōgun*, *Ieyasu*. *Nippō* line *Nichirin* express train south from *Ōita* to *Usuki* (28 mins), then 20 mins by taxi/bus or 30 mins by bicycle (available at the station).

3. *Yufuin* 湯布院

An *onsen* (hot-spring) resort town in the mountains near *Ōita*. Train from *Ōita* (1 hr 5 mins).

4. *Beppu* 別府

A large *onsen* (hot-spring) resort town 8 mins north of *Ōita* by train. Brash and commercial, but interesting to wander around. Hot springs for bathing (*onsen*) and just looking at (*jigoku* or 'hells'). The *onsen* are in the town, the *jigoku* a bus ride from the station.

Usuki Stone Buddha Statues

Further off

From **Nobeoka** station (1 hr 53 mins south of Ōita on *Nichirin* express train) there is a bus to **Takachiho** (1 hr 35 mins (more scenic route) or 1 hr 18 mins), according to legend the place where the sun goddess (*Amaterasu*) sent her grandson to rule over Japan. The first emperor (*Jimmu*) was said to have been his great-grandson. *Takachiho* is well known for performances of ancient *yokagura* dance, as well as for its gorge.

Aso Geopark (see *Kumamoto*: 'Places to visit nearby' p. 107). The JR *Hōhi* line runs from *Ōita* to *Aso* station in about 2 hrs.

To reach **Nagasaki**, take the *Nippō* line north to *Kokura* (1 hr 20 mins) and change for the *shinkansen* to *Hakata* (*Fukuoka*) (17 mins). Change there for *Nagasaki* (2 hrs). See *Fukuoka*: 'Further off' (p. 102) for more suggestions near *Nagasaki*.

For **Kumamoto** (major castle) and **Kagoshima** (southern *Kyūshū*), also take the *Nippō* line to *Kokura*. Change there for the *shinkansen* through to final destinations (see *Kumamoto* section p. 106). (There is a direct *Ōita-Kumamoto* line, but at the time of writing parts are still closed following an earthquake in 2016.)

One other possibility for onward travel is to take a ferry to **Shikoku** (the smallest of Japan's four main islands) from *Beppu* (8 mins north of *Ōita* by train, plus 15-min. bus to ferry terminal), or from *Usuki* (28 mins south of *Ōita* by *Nichirin* express, plus 10-min walk to ferry terminal). See 'Places to visit nearby' p.104.

熊本 *Kumamoto*

The place

Kumamoto is the capital and largest city (pop. 740,000) of *Kumamoto* Prefecture in south-west *Kyūshū*. It is home to one of Japan's greatest castles, which is being restored following earthquake damage in 2016.

Getting there

Air: *Aso Kumamoto* Airport is 1 hr by bus from *Kumamoto* station. The airport has flights from the *Tōkyō* area (*Narita*; *Haneda*), *Ōsaka* (*Itami*; *Kankū* – *Kansai* International) and *Nagoya* (*Chūbu* – Centrair; *Komaki*). Alternative airport: *Fukuoka* (bus 1 hr 55 mins).

Train: *Kumamoto* is on the *Kyūshū shinkansen* connecting to *Tōkyō* and intermediate stations through *Hakata* (*Fukuoka*). Journey times include *Hakata* (*Fukuoka*): 40 mins; *Hiroshima*: 1 hr 46 mins; *Shin-Kōbe*:3 hrs; *Shin-Ōsaka*: 3 hrs 13 mins; *Kyōto*: 3 hrs 57 mins; *Nagoya*: 4 hrs 50 mins; *Shin-Yokohama*: 6 hrs 16 mins; *Tōkyō*: 6 hrs 35 mins. If coming from *Ōita*, the quickest way currently is to take the *Nippō* line north to *Kokura* (1 hr 20 mins) and change there for the *shinkansen* to *Kumamoto*.

The stadium

Kumamoto Stadium (capacity 32,000) is 50 mins by bus from *Kumamoto* station. For domestic sporting events, buses often run from *Hikarinomori* station (20 mins by *Hōhi* main line from *Kumamoto* plus 15 mins by bus to stadium). The stadium is 10–15 mins by taxi from *Kumamoto* Airport. Otherwise known as the *Egao Kenkō* (Smile Health) Stadium, it is the home of *Roasso Kumamoto* FC.

Places to go nearby

1. *Kumamoto* Castle 熊本城

One of Japan's finest castles, it was badly damaged by the earthquake in 2016. At the time of writing, there was no admission to any buildings, but a walk around the perimeter is still very interesting. Reached from *Kumamoto* station by tram or castle loop bus (15 mins).

2. *Suizenji Jōjuen* Garden 水前寺成趣園

A pleasant Japanese garden dating from the 18th century. Tea house overlooking a lake. 30-min tram ride from *Kumamoto* station.

3. *Aso* Geopark 阿蘇ジオパーク

A UNESCO global geopark centred on Mount *Aso*, the volcano with the largest active crater in the world. The 2016 earthquake damaged the train line from *Kumamoto*, but bus services run from *Kumamoto* to *Aso* JR station (2 hrs), from where you can approach the caldera by a combination of buses (35 mins + 10 mins). Access depends on volcanic activity levels, so check for latest information before setting out.

Further off

Take the *shinkansen* further south to **Kagoshima** (57 mins to *Kagoshima Chūō* station). Major points of interest include *Sakurajima*, the volcano that sits across the bay from the city (15 mins by ferry), the *Sengan-en* garden (including World Heritage 19th-century industrial remnants) and the Museum of *Meiji* Restoration. From *Kagoshima* you can take a train on to the hot-spring town of **Ibusuki** (51 mins from *Kagoshima Chūō*), and try a sand bath.

Aso Geopark

Ferry services run from *Kumamoto* port to **Shimabara** port (30/60 mins). Buses run from the port to the town (*samurai* houses, street waterways). This is also a possible route if travelling to **Nagasaki**, though a more straightforward alternative is to take the *shinkansen* north to *Shin-Tosu*, and change for the express to *Nagasaki* (2hrs 21 mins).

The *Shimabara* Peninsula is home to **Mt Unzen**, which, with neighbouring islands, makes up the **Unzen Amakusa National Park**. *Unzen* village can be reached by bus from *Shimabara* or *Nagasaki*.

Amakusa is a group of islands close to the *Kumamoto* coast, where you can watch dolphins (at *Futae*) and visit fishing villages in which Christianity survived prohibition (17th–19th centuries). A group of such sites in *Amakusa* and *Nagasaki* have World Heritage status.

The *Shimabara* rebellion (1637–8) by mainly Christian peasants, is considered a major reason behind the subsequent strict prohibition of Christianity and the 200-year policy of national isolation.

The *Amakusa* islands can be visited by bus – 2 hrs 20 mins from *Kumamoto* station to *Amakusa Hondo* Bus Center. The bigger islands are connected by bridges. Another route to the *Amakusa* islands is by train and boat, via the World Heritage **Misumi West Port**, a 19th-century port built to service the vast (no longer in use) *Miike* Coal Mine between *Kumamoto* and *Fukuoka*. Take the *Misumi* JR line from *Kumamoto* to *Misumi* (52 mins). From *Misumi* West Port there is a boat to *Matsushima*. (17 mins).

The World Heritage *Manda* pit section of the **Miike coal mine** can be reached from *Kumamoto* by train (*Kagoshima* main line) to *Arao* (44 mins) plus 7-min taxi ride. *Miike* was very important in Japan's industrial development. It was also a mine that relied on convict labour, and in the Second World War included a POW camp (*Fukuoka* 17) holding US, Australian, Dutch and British prisoners who worked in the mine and nearby zinc foundry, along with forced labour from Korea and China. The POW camp was at the nearby *Miyahara* pit (3 km from *Ōmuta* station – bicycle, taxi, or bus plus 10-min walk. *Ōmuta* is one stop (3 mins) north of *Arao* on the *Kagoshima* main line.)

Onaka pe'ko pe'ko! (I'm starving!)

One major priority outside the stadium has to be food, so let's go and get something to eat.

First we'll see what types of restaurant there are and where to find them, then let's go inside one – in Japanese.

What's the choice?

Shokudō A simple and cheap type of restaurant, serving set meals (*teishoku*) with fish or meat plus rice, pickles and *miso* soup. Signs outside the restaurant are likely to include the words 食堂 (*shokudō*) or 食事処 (*shokuji-dokoro*). They often display plastic models of dishes by the entrance. This kind of display is very helpful, as English-language menus are not generally to be expected.

Speciality restaurants focusing on particular types of Japanese food: *sushi*, *tempura*, *udon*, *soba*, *yakitori*, etc. (see A–Z **p.118**).
Look for these words in the signs:

すし　寿し　寿司　(*sushi*)

てんぷら　天ぷら　天麩羅　(*tempura*)

うどん　(*udon*)

そば　蕎麦　(*soba*)

やきとり　焼鳥　(*yakitori*)

Tachigui These are cheap stand-up restaurants and stalls, most often specialising in *udon* うどん and *soba* そば. Sometimes you'll see them on station platforms. You'll notice a *tachigui* place by the rows of straight legs under the entrance curtain. At these and some other types of cheap restaurants meals are often paid for in advance at ticket machines near the entrance.

Izakaya Drinking places that serve Japanese dishes. They're often referred to as 'Japanese-style pubs', but people don't generally drink without ordering food of some kind. The word 居酒屋 may be written vertically on the red *chōchin* lanterns outside. On sitting down, you will often be served a small appetiser, for which you will be charged whether you want it or not. It's a kind of cover charge.

Ryōtei High-class Japanese cuisine. Rather like a club, sometimes you can't get in without being recommended. You'll see the word 料亭 discreetly displayed outside.

Chūka (Chinese) Very common. Look for 中華 on the sign.

Rāmen Look for the word ラーメン or らーめん on the sign.

Continental European Italian and French restaurants are quite common.

Look for these words on the signs:

イタリア料理 (*itaria ryōri* Italian cuisine)

フランス料理 (*furansu ryōri* French cuisine)

'Family' restaurants Not just for families, these serve a range of Western, Japanese and Chinese dishes, with photos on the menu. Leading chains include: Gusto (**ガスト**), Denny's (**デニーズ**), Royal Host (**ロイヤルホスト**).

Fast food McDonald's, Kentucky Fried Chicken, etc. are common. The most prominent Japanese hamburger chain is Mos Burger (**モスバーガー**). Others that could be classified as Japanese fast food (though not takeaway) include *gyūdon* (see *domburi*, p.118) chains (*Yoshinoya/Sukiya*) and Japanese curry chains (CoCo *Ichibanya*). (NB: Japanese curry is normally very mild.)

If you're after a snack, convenience stores (*kombini*) are useful. You can get a range of snacks and drinks, as well as ready-to-eat meals. They are found almost everywhere and often open 24 hours. Chain names include: 7-Eleven (**セブンイレブン**), Sunkus (**サンクス**), Family Mart (**ファミリーマート**) and Lawson (**ローソン**).

Supermarkets (**スーパー** *sūpā*) are cheaper and have a better selection, especially of fresh food, but they can be few and far between in the bigger cities. Department store basements normally sell ready-to-eat delicacies.

Stations often have a range of snack and *bentō* (boxed meal) outlets. Many *shinkansen* and some other long-distance trains have trolley services.

Where are the restaurants?

Stations (駅 *eki*) There are likely to be restaurants in or near stations, at least in the larger towns. If it's a big station, there may be an area for restaurants on an upper floor of the station building. You'll normally find glass cabinets outside these restaurants displaying models of what's on offer and how much it costs. A lot of big stations link to underground malls – another good place to find restaurants. Sometimes you'll find noodle stalls on station platforms.

Streets Larger Japanese towns generally have a shopping/ entertainment area referred to as *hankagai*. You'll find *izakaya* here, and often Chinese, Italian and French restaurants. You'll find *shokudō* and Japanese speciality restaurants too, but some of these are likely to close quite early.

Department stores These normally have a number of restaurants on an upper floor. Most department stores also have basements where ready-to-eat delicacies can be bought.

Hotels Larger hotels will have restaurants, of course, though they will often be expensive. Some smaller hotels also have restaurants, and these can sometimes offer good value.

Big shopping malls The malls themselves may be hard to find without a car. But they often have food courts similar to those in other countries. Easy to order and cheap.

Roadside There are also plenty of large restaurants on major motor traffic routes. This is where most 'family' restaurants will be found.

Closing times

Izakaya and some restaurants stay open late, but don't bank on finding places to eat easily after 8pm in provincial areas. Station restaurants are likely to close by 9pm.

Okay, it's time to throw caution to the wind and approach a restaurant:

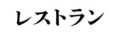

(*resutoran*)

Visiting a restaurant – step by step

Step 1 Is it open?

Here is a sign that gives the game away:

(open)

If it's closed, you may see one of the following:

| 本日閉店 | 本日休業 | 準備中 |

Step 2 Getting to your seats

Once you're inside a member of staff will say:

Irassha'ima'se!

(Welcome!)

You may then be asked:

Nan-mei sama desu ka?

(How many people?)

Here's how to count people – one to six:

one: *hitori*	two: *futari*
three: *san-nin*	four: *yo'nin*
five: *go-nin*	six: *roku-nin*

112

If you want a no-smoking table say:

Ki(n)'en seki o'nega'i shimasu

(A no-smoking table, please)

You'll be shown to your table and given glasses of water (sometimes tea) and probably hot hand towels (*oshibori*) or disposable hand wipes.

You will be normally addressed as **o-kyaku-sama**, which could be translated as Honoured Customer, but don't take it too personally.

Step 3 Ordering

In taking your order the waiting staff may say:

O-no'mimono wa?

Drinks?)

O-kimari deshō ka?

(Have you decided?)

(It's perfectly normal not to order drinks, by the way.)

If you want assistance at any time, say:

Sumima'sen!

(Excuse me!)

Step 4 Eating

Before starting to eat say: **Itada'kimasu**

Well, you don't have to say that, but Japanese people do!

'Itada'kimasu' is a humble expression meaning 'I/we receive'.

Food etiquette

When having Japanese- or Chinese-style food:

- You can lift a bowl to your mouth and drink directly from it.
- You can lift plates towards your mouth to make life easier when using chopsticks.
- You can make a slurping sound when eating noodles.
- You can pick up *sushi* with your fingers.
- Don't stick your chopsticks into your food and leave them there.
- Don't pass anything from one set of chopsticks to another.

Step 5 Leaving

Japanese people usually tidy up a bit before leaving – putting everything on the tray, lids in place, chopsticks partially back in their little paper envelopes, napkins folded.

You normally pay at the exit when leaving, so you don't usually have to ask for the bill.

Tips are not required or expected.

To say thank you for the meal, say:

Gochisō-sama!

(That was a great meal!)

But what about the food itself? On p. 118–24 you'll find our illustrated lists of Japanese dishes. Before that, on the next three pages, you'll find some general food-related words. But first a note on vegetarian (**ベジタリアン** *bejitarian*) and vegan (**ビーガン** *bīgan*) food:

Vegetarian/vegan food

It's not easy to find restaurants in Japan that cater for vegetarianism or veganism, particularly outside the biggest cities. Traditional Buddhist monastery food (*shōjin ryōri*) is vegetable-based, though, and it is possible to stay at certain temples.

MEALS

breakfast	*asa-gohan* (literally: morning rice/meal); *chōshoku*
lunch	*hiru-gohan* (literally: midday rice/meal); *chūshoku*
supper	*yū-gohan/ban-gohan* (literally: evening rice/meal); *yūshoku*
buffet-style	*ba'ikingu* バイキング
set meal	*setto* セット (or) *teishoku*
individual dish	*tampin*
main course	*mein* メイン
dessert	*dezāto* デザート

('Starters' are not a normal element in a Japanese meal. Soup, when served, will normally accompany the main course.)

FOODS

apple	*ringo*
banana	*banana* バナナ
beef	*gyū-niku*
bread	*pan* パン
carrot	*ninjin*
cheese	*chīzu* チーズ
chicken	*tori-niku*
chips	*fura'ido-po'teto* フライドポテト
crisps	*po'teto-chippsu* ポテトチップス
curry	*karē* カレー
egg	*tamago*
fish	*sakana*
fruit	*kudamono*
meat	*niku*
noodles	*menrui*
onion	*tama'negi*

orange	*orenji* オレンジ (or) *mikan*
pepper (spice)	*koshō*
pepper (veg)	*pīman* ピーマン
pork	*buta-niku*
potato	*jaga-imo*
prawn	*ebi*
rice	*gohan*
salad	*sarada* サラダ
salt	*shio*
sandwich	*sando'icchi* サンドイッチ
soup	*sūpu* スープ
spaghetti	*supagetti* スパゲッティ
spinach	*hōrensō*
spring onion	*ne'gi*
steak	*sutēki* ステーキ
stew	*shichū* シチュー
tomato	*tomato* トマト
vegetable	*yasa'i*

RESTAURANTS

table	*tēburu* テーブル
counter	*kauntā* カウンター
chair	*isu*
menu	*menyū* メニュー
no-smoking seat	*ki(n)'en seki*
chopsticks	*hashi*
knife	na'ifu ナイフ
fork	*fōku* フォーク
spoon	*supūn* スプーン

paper napkin	*napukin* ナプキン
hot hand towel	*oshibori*
bill/check	*okanjō; oka'ikei*

PORTION SIZES (rice)

small helping	*komori* 小盛
large helping	*ōmori* 大盛

DESCRIPTIONS

tasty	*oishii*
looks tasty	*oishisō*
I love (it)	*da'i'suki* (can be used for people too)
unpleasant taste	*mazui*
I don't like it much	*amari suki ja na'i*
sweet	*ama'i*
hot (spicy)	*kara'i*
salty	*kara'i/shoppa'i*
bitter	*niga'i*
sharp	*suppa'i*
fresh	*shinsen*
good smell	*ii nioi*
hot (temperature)	*atsui*
cold	*tsumeta'i*

POLITE PHRASES BEFORE AND AFTER FOOD

(before eating)	*itada'kimasu* (I/we receive.)
(after eating)	*gochisō-sama* (That was a great meal.)

Japanese foods

If you don't know your *soba* from your *sukiyaki*, this is for you. *Aiko* and her friends' illustrated guide to Japanese food comes in two parts:

1. A–Z of foods that are common around the country.
2. Speciality dishes from World Cup cities and regions.

A–Z of Japanese foods	
bentō 	A packed ready-to-eat meal. *Bentōs* are sold at convenience stores, *bentō* shops, stations and on some trains. Many stations (*eki*) have their own local speciality *bentōs*, known as *eki-ben*.
domburi/...don 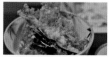 tendon ▲  oyakodon ▲	A large bowl of rice with some other type of food on top. For example: *Gyūdon*: rice topped with simmered slices of beef with onion. *Katsudon*: rice topped with pork fried in breadcrumbs, and egg. *Tendon*: rice topped with *tempura*. *Oyakodon*: rice topped with chicken and egg. ('*Oya*' means 'parent' and '*ko*' means 'child')
kon'nyaku 	A firm, jelly-like substance made from konjac yam tubers. Used as *o'den* and as noodles with *sukiyaki* and *gyūdon* (see *domburi* above).
manjū 	A confection with *azuki* red bean paste in a soft coating made from wheat or rice flour and other ingredients.

miso-shiru (miso soup) 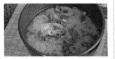	Clear soup made with *miso* paste, often with *waka'me* seaweed and *tōfu*. Frequently served as part of a set meal (see *teishoku*) together with rice and fish/meat.
mochi 	Rice paste that is much used in confectionery, often filled with *anko* (*azuki* bean paste). Words for the different types of such confection end with 'mochi'. For example: *Sakura-mochi* ('cherry blossom *mochi*'), normally eaten in spring.
nattō 	Fermented soy beans, often served with rice for breakfast. Sticky, and difficult to pick up with chopsticks, but worth trying.
nori 	Seaweed formed into sheets. Uses include wrapping *sushi* (*ma'ki-zushi*) and *onigiri*.
ocha'zuke 	Rice served in a bowl of Japanese tea. Often eaten at *izakaya* after drinking alcohol.
o'den 	Various foods that have been boiled in a light soy-flavoured broth. For example: eggs, *daikon* radish, *kon'nyaku*, *satsuma-age* fishcakes.
okonomiyaki 	A thick savoury pancake made with cabbage and other vegetables. Popular variants include: *Buta-tama* (contains pork and egg). *Ebi-tama* (contains prawn and egg). *Modan yaki* (contains *yakisoba*).

onigiri 	A rice ball – normally triangular when sold in shops. Usually wrapped in *nori* seaweed and containing something inside the rice, like a piece of salmon (*sa'ke*), or a pickled plum (*u'meboshi*).
rāmen 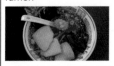	Wheat noodles in broth. Many towns/areas have their special types of *rāmen*. For example, *Hakata rāmen* from *Fukuoka*.
sashimi 	Raw sliced fish. The word *sashimi* can also be used to refer to raw sliced meat, but you are unlikely to encounter this at ordinary restaurants.
sembei 	Rice crackers, often served with tea.
shabushabu 	Thin-sliced meat boiled in a pot on the table with vegetables.
soba 	Thin buckwheat noodles. Served boiled, hot or cold. *Soba* is traditionally a mountain-area food and many mountain districts have their own speciality *soba*.
sukiyaki 	Thinly sliced beef fried and simmered in a shallow pan at the table with vegetables. Normally dipped into raw egg before being eaten.

sushi  *nigiri-zushi* ▲  *maki-zushi* ▲	*Sushi* is a combination of vinegared rice and fish, etc. It comes in various forms, for example: *Nigiri-zushi* – hand-compressed rice with fish, etc. on top. *Ma'ki-zushi* – rice and fish, etc. wrapped in seaweed. *Chirashi-zushi* – a bowl of vinegared rice with pieces of fish on top or mixed in. *Niku-zushi* uses raw meat rather than fish – but you won't find it in normal *sushi* outlets.
takoyaki 	Octopus in balls of batter. Often eaten as a snack.
teishoku 	Normally means that your food comes as a set with a bowl of rice, pickled vegetables (*tsu'kemono*) and some *miso* soup (*miso-shiru*).
tempura 	Fish, prawns, vegetables deep fried in a light batter. Like 'fish-and-chips'-style fish, it has its origins in Portugal.
teppanyaki 	Beef, seafood, noodles, etc. cooked on a hot metal plate at the diners' table/counter.
tōfu 	Soybean curd. Served in various guises. You may come across it as, for example, *hiya-yakko* (chilled with toppings, such as tuna flakes and spring onion) or *a'gedashi-dōfu* (hot *tōfu* fried in flour or potato starch, often served with a kelp- and fish-based stock).

tsu'kemono 	Pickled or fermented vegetables served in small bowls.
udon 	Thick wheat flour noodles. Served hot or cold, often in broth. Also served fried (*yaki-udon*).
u'meboshi 	Pickled plums.
wagashi 	Japanese-style confectionery, including *manjū* and *mochi*-based sweets.
yakisoba 	*Rāmen*-style wheat noodles fried with pork and vegetables.
yakitori 	Pieces of chicken and vegetable grilled on skewers.

World Cup venue *meibutsu*

Meibutsu are foods that are particularly associated with a local area, either because they have a long tradition of being produced there or because they have been developed specifically to represent or promote the area. The list includes some of *Aiko*'s family's favourites, which are not always (if ever) haut cuisine.

Host area	Appearance	What on earth is it?
札幌 *Sapporo*	スープカレー	***sūpu-karē*** Light curry-flavoured soup with meat and roasted vegetables.
釜石 *Kamaishi*	ひっつみ	***hittsumi*** Soy sauce broth with dough, chicken or fish, and vegetables.
熊谷 *Kumagaya*	いなり寿司	***inari-zushi*** Rolls of *sushi* rice in pouches of deep-fried *tōfu*.
東京 *Tōkyō*	柳川鍋	***Yanagawa-na'be*** Hotpot with loach, egg and vegetables. Served in an earthenware pot.
横浜 *Yokohama*	牛鍋	***gyūna'be*** A beef dish similar to *sukiyaki*, but with no frying. (Like rugby, beef-eating first came to Japan in the 19th Century through ports like *Yokohama*.)

静岡 *Shizuoka*	たまごふわふわ 	***tamago-fuwafuwa*** Egg soufflé over broth. A speciality of *Fukuroi* city, where *Shizuoka* Stadium Ecopa is located.
豊田 *Toyota*	へぼ料理 	***hebo ryōri*** Dishes made with wasp larvae.
東大阪 *Higashi-Ōsaka*	豚まん 	***butaman*** Pork-filled buns or dumplings.
神戸 *Kōbe*	明石焼き 	***Akashi-yaki*** Small dumplings made of egg-rich batter and octopus, dipped in thin fish broth.
福岡 *Fukuoka*	博多ラーメン 	***Hakata rāmen*** *Rāmen* noodles in pork-based broth topped with sliced pork belly.
大分 *Ōita*	とり天 	***tori-ten*** Chicken *tempura*.
熊本 *Kumamoto*	高菜めし 	***takana-meshi*** Rice with pickled mustard leaves.

Nodo kara kara! (I'm parched!)

Okay, let's get something to drink.

Doko? (Where?)

If you want to sit down with some **alcohol** (*osa'ke*), your options include the following:

***Bā* (bar)**   A hotel bar is one of the few places you can sit and drink without buying food. Look for the sign: バー (Bar). You'll find bars in the streets of big cities too. *Roppongi* in *Tōkyō* is one area where foreigners gather.

Izakaya   As mentioned in the Eat section (p. 109), *izakaya* are often referred to as Japanese-style pubs, but you will be expected to order at least some dishes of food and a cover charge usually applies (you will receive a small bowl of food on arrival and will be obliged to pay for it). You'll frequently see the word 居酒屋 (*izakaya*) outside, often on *aka-chōchin* red paper lanterns. See photo on p. 109.

Yakitori-ya   A *yakitori* place specialises in grilled skewered chicken, but is also good for downing beer and *sa'ke*. The signs outside will say 焼鳥 or やきとり (*yakitori*). Look through the window and you'll probably see chicken being grilled. You'll smell it too.

If you want to relax with some **coffee or tea** you can try:

Kissaten   These tend to be cosy, non-chain coffee/tea shops. Look for signs saying 喫茶 (*kissa*) or 珈琲 (*kōhī*).

Words like café will also often appear in alphabet or *katakana* カフェ (café).

Western-style coffee shops   Chains include Doutor (ドトール) and Starbucks (スターバックス).

If you want to take drinks with you:

Convenience stores (コンビニ *kombini*) are good places to pick up cans and bottles. You'll also find drinks at small shops/stands (*ba'iten*) at many **stations**. There are huge numbers of drink **vending machines** (*jihanki*) around the country. You can normally use a 1,000-yen note, as well as coins. Alcohol sales at street vending machines are not permitted after 11pm.

DRINKS

alcohol	*osa'ke* (used as a general word for alcohol, as well as specifically for Japanese rice wine)

beer
  draft beer
  bottled beer
	bīru ビール
	  nama bīru
	  bin bīru

bottle	*bin*
brandy	*burandē* ブランデー
coffee	*kōhī* コーヒー
cup	*kappu* カップ
glass (small)	*koppu* コップ
glass (tankard)	*jokki* ジョッキ
ice	*kōri*
iced coffee	*aisu-kōhī* アイスコーヒー
iced tea	*aisu-tī* アイスティー
lemon	*remon* レモン
milk	*miruku* ミルク
orange juice	*orenji-jūsu* オレンジジュース
soft drink (fruit juice or fruit-flavoured carbonated drinks)	*jūsu* ジュース
sugar	*satō*
tea (Indian – black)	*kōcha*
tea (Japanese/Chinese)	*ocha*
water – cold water – hot	*mizu* *oyu*
water – mineral	*mi'neraru-wōtā* ミネラルウォーター
whisky	*uisukī* ウイスキー

wine
  red wine
  white wine
	wa'in ワイン
	  aka-wa'in
	  shiro-wa'in

Japanese drinks

Tea

ocha	general word for any Japanese or Chinese tea
sencha	high-quality green tea
bancha	lower-quality green tea
hōjicha	roasted tea (brown)
maccha	powdered green tea
mugicha	barley infusion
ūroncha	partially fermented tea (Chinese, but drunk a lot in Japan)

Alcohol

sa'ke	made from rice; 15 per cent alcohol
shōchū	distilled liquor made from rice, sweet potatoes or other ingredients 25–35 per cent alcohol

Variants on coffee and black tea

amerikan アメリカン	a weakish coffee
burendo (blend) ブレンド	stronger than *amerikan*
miruku-tī (milk tea) ミルクティー	tea served with (often hot) milk
roiyaru-miruku-tī (royal milk tea) ロイヤルミルクティー	tea made with hot milk instead of water

Beer Choices

1. *nama* 生 = draft
   bin 瓶 = bottle
   kan 缶 = can
2. *da'i* 大 = large
   chū 中 = medium

Sa'ke Choices

kan = hot
hiya = cold

Key drinking expressions

Toria'ezu bīru (*Beer for now*) When people gather for a drink they almost always agree to start with lager-style beer. When someone comes to take their order they'll say: *Toria'ezu bīru*.

Kampa'i! (Cheers!)

Uma'i! (That tastes good!)

Women are more likely to use the word: **Oishii!** (same meaning.)

Mō ippon! (Another bottle!)

Mō ippa'i! (Another glass/cup!)

Ikki! (Down in one! – chant *'ikki' 'ikki'* as the drinker drinks.)

Mō jūbun. (That's enough.)

Yopparatta! (I'm drunk!)

Sumima'sen! (I'm sorry!)

Hontō-ni sumima'sen! (I'm really sorry!)

Of course you don't have to drink alcohol. Just say:

Osa'ke wa nomima'sen (I don't drink alcohol.)

Drinking etiquette

- If drinking with Japanese people, wait for everybody in the group to have a drink in front of them before starting.
- Somebody will say *kampa'i* and then everybody raises their glasses and takes a sip.
- With bottled beer or flasks of *sa'ke*, people normally fill up each other's glass or cup. When having your glass filled, it's polite to lift it towards the flask or bottle.
- You normally don't leave until others decide to go. It's a group decision, like birds taking flight.
- There's no tradition of buying rounds. When people go out drinking, the bill is often split equally (*warikan*), or someone senior may pay for everything. With visitors to Japan, Japanese people will often like to act as hosts.

Nemui! (I'm sleepy!)

Time for bed.

First, a brief summary of some of the main types of accommodation. Then we'll check in at a hotel – in Japanese.

Seven types of accommodation

(There are others, of course, but these are common.)

International hotels

- Available in the biggest cities and at airports.
- Like big hotels in any country.

Business hotels (ビジネスホテル *bijinesu hoteru*)

- Cheaper than international hotels.
- Available in all towns and cities.
- Rooms and beds can be small, especially single (シングル *shinguru*) or semi-double (セミダブル *semidaburu*).
- The en-suite bathrooms may often feel cramped, with a small bath-tub to crouch in. Sometimes these hotels also have communal bathrooms (大風呂 *ōburo* or 大浴場 *daiyokujō*).
- Breakfast is normally available. It may range from coffee and toast to a substantial buffet.
- This type of hotel often has coin-operated washing machines and driers (*koin randorī* コインランドリー)

Capsule hotels (カプセルホテル *kapuseru hoteru*)

- A horizontal compartment in which you can lie down but not stand up. Cheap accommodation in big cities.

Ryokan (旅館)

- Tea will often be prepared for you in your room when you arrive.
- You will normally have your own bathroom, but one of the attractions of a *ryokan* is often the communal bath, frequently partly outside (*rotenburo* 露天風呂).
- Japanese-style dinner and breakfast, often served in your room.
- Sleeping in a *futon* on a *tatami* mat floor. The *futons* are kept in a cupboard in the room and will be prepared for you after you arrive.
- Service is included, but some guests who feel especially well looked after leave about 10% of the room charge in clean notes in an envelope in the room. This is normally only done at very traditional establishments.

Minshuku (民宿)

- Like a *ryokan*, but smaller and cheaper – more 'at-home'.

Guest House (ゲストハウス *gesto ha'usu*)

- Normally hostel-type accommodation, often with shared rooms and kitchen facilities.

Minpaku (民泊)

- Airbnb-type arrangements. A variety of accommodation in big cities and tourist spots.

Okay let's go into a hotel:

ホテル

(*hoteru*)

When you go into a hotel the receptionist will say:

Irassha'ima'se!

(Welcome!)

If you have been kept waiting so much as a second, and often if you haven't been waiting at all, they will say:

Omata'se itashimashita.

(We have kept you waiting.)

If necessary, you can attract attention by saying:

Sumima'sen!

(Excuse me!)

If you have a reservation, you can say:

[Your surname] *desu.*   (I am X.)

Yoyaku shimashita.   (I have a reservation.)

(For effective communication, say your name slowly and clearly, and try to base it on Japanese pronunciation – never forget the Vowel Haka....)

The receptionist will repeat your name, adding the polite suffix *sama*, and give details of your reservation:

Type of room

single	*shinguru* (シングル)
semi-double	*semidaburu* (セミダブル)
double	*daburu* (ダブル)
twin	*tsuin* (ツイン)

Number of people (using the polite way of counting guests)

one: *o-hitori-sama/ ichi-mei sama*	two: *o-futari-sama/ni-mei sama*

Number of nights

one: *ippaku*	two: *ni-haku*
three: *sampaku*	four: *yompaku*
five: *go-haku*	six: *roppaku*

If you want a non-smoking room say:

Ki(n)'en-shitsu o'nega'i shimasu.

(A no-smoking room, please.)

(Warning: if you are irritated by the smell of tobacco in bedrooms, it is strongly recommended that you choose a no-smoking room at the reservation stage.)

The receptionist will ask you to fill in a registration form and to show your passport. Then you will be told your room number, given your room key (**kagi**) and shown the elevator (**erebētā エレベーター**).

If you want to check what floor your room is, you can say:

(Heya wa) nan-ka'i desu ka?

(What floor (is the room)?)

first (ground) floor: *ikka'i*	second floor: *ni-ka'i*
third floor: *san-ga'i*	fourth floor: *yon-ka'i*
fifth floor: *go-ka'i*	sixth floor: *rokka'i*

If you want to ask when breakfast is, say:

> *Chōshoku wa nan-ji kara desu ka?*

(When is breakfast from?)

> *(Chōshoku wa) nan-ji ma'de desu ka?*

(When is it (breakfast) until?)

NB: If breakfast is 'until 9am', that means that guests will be expected to have vacated their tables by 9am. So if you want anything to eat, don't wait till the last minute.

If you want to confirm check-out time, you can say:

> *Chekku-a'uto wa nan-ji ma'de desu ka?*

(What's the latest check-out time?)

NB: If you're still in your room at check-out time, expect a prompt call from reception. You may be asked to pay extra.

Other useful expressions

stairs	*kaidan* 階段
emergency exit	*hijōguchi* 非常口
reception	*furonto* フロント
room service	*rūmu-sābisu* ルームサービス

Leaving and forwarding luggage

If you want to leave your luggage at reception after you have checked out, you can say:

> *Nimotsu o azu'ke'te'mo ii desu ka?*
>
> (Can I leave my luggage?)

You can often send your luggage on. The service is referred to as *takuha'i-sābisu*. To ask if a hotel has this service you can say:

> *Takuha'i-sābisu arimasu-ka?*
>
> (Do you have a luggage-forwarding service?)

The easiest type of shop to find is a
convenience store *kombini* (コンビニ).
These are good for getting drinks and
snacks and ready-to-eat meals. Supermarkets
are cheaper and have more fresh food, but
they're not so easy to find, especially in big cities.

Let's pop into a shop – in Japanese:

1. The automatic door is likely to fly open before you expect it to.

2. When you get inside someone (or a recorded voice) will say:

   Irassha'ima'se! (Welcome!)

3. To ask whether the shop has something:

   Sumima'sen. (Excuse me.)

   X arimasu ka? (Do you have X?)

   Arigatō. (Thank you.)

4. To ask how much something is:

   Sumima'sen. (Excuse me.)

   Ikura desu ka? (How much is it/this?)

   Arigatō. (Thank you.)

5. To ask what something is:

   Sumima'sen. (Excuse me.)

   Nan desu ka? (What is it/this?)

   Arigatō. (Thank you.)

6. When you get to the front of the queue the cashier will say:

   Omata'se itashimashita. (Sorry to keep you waiting.)

7. The cashier will probably put your purchases in a plastic bag.
   If you don't want one, say:

   Fukuro wa ii desu. (I don't want a bag.)

8. The shop may well not accept credit/debit cards.

9. Consumption tax will normally be added at the till, making the price less round than you might have expected.

10. Your change will be piled into your open hand, notes first making it easy to drop all the coins on the floor.

11. When you eventually pick them up and look ready to leave, the cashier will say:

   Arigatō goza'imashita! (Thank you! – Extra polite.)

   Mata okoshi kudasa'ima'se. (Please come again.)

12. Most Japanese customers don't say 'thank you' in a shop.

   But you can of course! **Arigatō!**

SHOPS, etc.

shop	mi'se/shoppu ショップ
supermarket	sūpā スーパー
convenience store	kombini コンビニ
department store	depāto デパート
post office	yūbinkyoku
bank	ginkō
tourist information	kankō-an'na'ijo
I don't want a bag	fukuro wa ii desu

Even if your country doesn't win the World Cup, good behaviour from fans will win it the favour of your hosts.
So here are a few tips:

In the street

- Don't eat or drink while walking down the street.
- Don't sit on the pavement.

Footwear

Okay: CONCENTRATE!

- In a traditional Japanese-style space (a home, a Japanese inn, a temple, etc.) you take your shoes off at the entrance and put on some slippers (*surippa* スリッパ). The slippers are provided. If you have big feet, they may only cover a few toes. Don't let that put you off.
- If you go on to a *tatami* mat (traditional thick straw mat used as indoor flooring) anywhere, take off your slippers or shoes first. Only walk on *tatami* in socks/bare feet.
- Try not to let your bare or stockinged feet touch the outside floor when taking off shoes/slippers.
- Having taken off your shoes/slippers, arrange them neatly on the floor, with toes pointing outwards. Or if there are shoe shelves, place them there. (At some sightseeing spots you will be given plastic bags to carry your shoes in as you look around a building.)
- When you go to the lavatory, you may find some special slippers there. Take off your house slippers and put on the other slippers. Make sure not to take the house slippers into the lavatory, and not to take the lavatory slippers out.

In view of all the shoe removal that goes on, you may prefer NEVER to go out in Japan wearing socks that could cause embarrassment, especially not socks with holes in them.

Also, it can save quite a bit of awkward wobbling if you have footwear that can be slipped easily on and off in a confined space.

Baths

A lot of hotels and inns have communal baths. The vital point is that the water in the bath should be kept clean.

- Wash yourself and rinse away all soap etc. before getting into the (sometimes fiendishly hot) water.
- You will find places to sit and wash in the communal bathroom. (Rinse down your stool and bowl after use.)
- Do not swim around in the bath or put your head underwater.
- Bring your own towels (the towels from your hotel room – one large, one small). You are unlikely to find spare towels in the changing room.
- Take a small towel into the bathroom with you and dry yourself off before going back into the changing room.
- Don't put the small towel in the bath water. If you want to keep it with you while you are in the water, you can fold it and put it on your head.
- Many people wear their *yukata* (cotton robe provided by the accommodation) on their way to the bathroom. You don't have to do this, though it is normal in a *ryokan* (Japanese-style inn).

Other situations

See p. 67 (trains); p. 114 (eating); p. 128 (drinking).

Credit cards

Things are changing, but Japan is still primarily
a cash society. So always be ready to pay cash
at restaurants and shops.

To ask if you can use a card, say:

Kādo de ii desu ka? (Is a card okay?)

Cash dispensers

A lot of cash dispensers do not accept foreign cards. However,
those at post offices and 7-Eleven convenience stores do.

See below for lists of cards they accept according to websites
Jan. 2019:

Post offices (Japan Post Bank)
Visa; VisaElectron; PLUS; Mastercard; Maestro; Cirrus;
American Express; JCB; China Unionpay; Discover.

7-Eleven
Visa; Mastercard; UnionPay; American Express; JCB; Discover;
Diners Club.

Currency exchange

Post offices and major banks can exchange money, though the
process can be time-consuming and there may be problems
with lesser-known currencies. US$ is likely to be the most
straightforward. There are no currency exchange-specific
businesses in the streets, as are found in tourist spots in other
countries. There are facilities at international airports, though.

To ask to change money say:

Ryōga'e o'nega'i shimasu. (Currency exchange, please.)

Consumption tax (*shōhizei*)

Prices displayed in shops do not generally include consumption tax, meaning that when you buy something, you often end up with small coins as change. The rate of tax is due to rise at the beginning of October 2019, from 8% to 10%.

MONEY-RELATED WORDS	
bank	*ginkō*
currency exchange	*ryōga'e*
cash dispenser	ATM (*ē-tī-emu* エーティーエム)
cash	*genkin*
note	*osatsu*
coin	*koin* コイン
credit card	*kurejitto-kādo* クレジットカード
debit card	*debitto-kādo* デビットカード
pay (verb)	*harau*
bill/check	*okanjō; oka'ikei*
consumption tax	*shōhizei*
change	*otsuri*
receipt	*ryōshūshō* (written receipt) *reshīto* レシート (till receipt)

For currency names see p. 41.

Japanese coins and notes

 ichi-en (1 yen)	go-en (5 yen)
jū-en (10 yen)	go-jū-en (50 yen)
hyaku-en (100 yen)	go-hyaku-en (500 yen)
se(n)-en (1,000 yen)	go-se(n)-en (5,000 yen)
ichi-ma(n)-en (10,000 yen)	

It is best to keep a good supply of 100-yen coins for use in coin lockers and coin laundries.

Police can be found at street-side police stations called *kōban* 交番. Many have KOBAN in alphabet at the entrance. They are often small detached buildings.

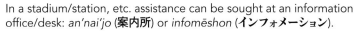

Emergency telephone numbers:

    Ambulance and fire: 119

    Police: 110

In a stadium/station, etc. assistance can be sought at an information office/desk: *an'nai'jo* (**案内所**) or *infomēshon* (**インフォメーション**).

GENERAL PHRASES

Please help me!	*tasu'ke'te kudasa'i*
Help!	*tasu'ke'te!*
I have a problem	*komatte imasu*
Can you speak English?	*eigo dekimasu-ka?*
I don't understand Japanese	*nihongo wakarima'sen*
I don't understand	*wakarima'sen*
I don't know	*wakarima'sen*
Excuse me	*sumima'sen*
I'm sorry	*sumima'sen*

ILLNESS/INJURY

it hurts	*ita'i*
ill	*byōki*
itchy	*kayui*
allergy	*a'rerugī* **アレルギー**
collapsed	*tao're'ta*

DAMAGE/MALFUNCTION

broken down/faulty	*koshō shita*
broken	*kowa're'ta*
spilt	*koboshita*

EVENTS

accident	*jiko*
earthquake	*jishin*
typhoon	*ta'ifū*
fire	*kaji*
evacuation	*hinan*
thief	*dorobō/suri (pickpocket)*

SERVICES

the police	*keisatsu*
policeman	*omawari-san; keisatsu-kan*
ambulance	*kyūkyūsha*
doctor	*isha*
hospital/clinic	*byōin*
dentist	*ha'isha*
embassy	*ta'ishikan*
interpreter	*tsūyaku*

LOST

I'm lost	*michi ni mayotta*
I can't find my wife* (for words for other relatives/friends see p. 18)	*tsuma* ga mitsukarana'i*
I've lost (a thing)	*X o nakushita*
I left (something)	*X o wasureta*

POSSESSIONS

camera	*ka'mera* カメラ
mobile phone; smart phone	*keita'i; sumaho* スマホ
i pad	*a'i-paddo* アイパッド
laptop computer	*pasokon* パソコン
bag	*kaban; baggu* バッグ
suitcase	*sūtsukēsu* スーツケース
back pack	*ryukku* リュック
luggage	*nimotsu*
glasses	*mega'ne*
sunglasses	*sangurasu* サングラス
umbrella	*kasa*
coat	*kōto* コート
clothes	*yōfuku*
hat	*bōshi*
jacket	*jaketto* ジャケット
wallet	*sa'ifu*
watch/clock	*tokei*
pen	*pen* ペン
passport	*pasupōto* パスポート
ticket	train/bus: *kippu* For a plane/match, many people say: *chiketto* チケット

Earthquakes, *Tsunami* and Typhoons

The JNTO (Japan National Tourism Organisation) provides information on action to be taken in the event of emergencies such as earthquakes, *tsunami* and extreme weather.
https://www.jnto.go.jp/safety-tips/eng/emergency/index.html

No area in Japan is safe from earthquakes and any low-lying area near the coast, including river valleys, could be affected by *tsunami*.

The main typhoon (storms with very strong winds and heavy rain) season lasts from the summer to early autumn.

Some common Emergency Refuge signs

Refuge
(Place)

Tsunami Refuge
(Place)

Tsunami Refuge
(Building)

Refuge signs may have English on them. The English wordings may not be the same as those given above.

Souvenirs Japan-style – *Omiya'ge*

When they go on a trip, Japanese people always buy something to take home. These are called *omiya'ge*. Traditional *omiya'ge* include Japanese treats like *manjū* and *sembei* (see Food A–Z p. 118), but Western-style foods are also popular, including cheese-cake and crème caramel (what the Japanese call *purin*). You'll often find *omiya'ge* for sale at railway stations. Of course, souvenirs don't have to be edible, but for Japanese people they very often are!

Besides their love of rugby, *Aiko*'s whole family, including the head coach, share an interest in patisserie, as well as snacks in general. Here, they give their selection of *omiya'ge* from around the 2019 rugby host regions.

Host area	Appearance	What on earth is it?
札幌 *Sapporo*	マルセイバター サンド	***maru'sei batā sando*** A soft biscuit with a cream filling made with white chocolate, raisins and *Hokkaidō* butter.
釜石 *Kamaishi*	南部せんべい	***Nambu sembei*** Wheat crackers. Can be sweet or savoury. They are often flavoured with sesame seeds or peanuts. *Nambu* (southern part) is an old name for the region.
熊谷 *Kumagaya*	五家宝	***gokabō*** Rolls of crunchy, sweetened white rice wrapped in soybean flour (*kinako*).
東京 *Tōkyō*	雷おこし	***kaminari okoshi*** Sweetened crispy rice, often flavoured with peanuts.

横浜 *Yokohama*	月餅 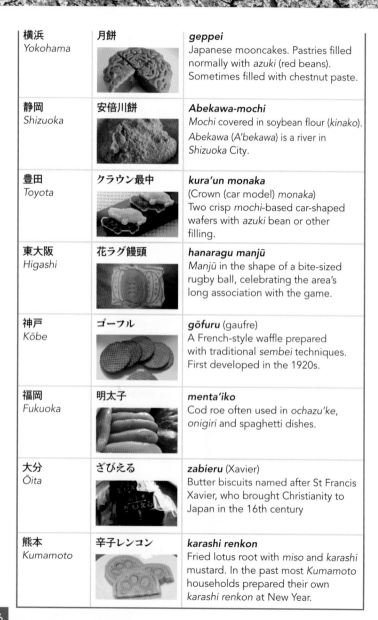	***geppei*** Japanese mooncakes. Pastries filled normally with *azuki* (red beans). Sometimes filled with chestnut paste.
静岡 *Shizuoka*	安倍川餅	***Abekawa-mochi*** *Mochi* covered in soybean flour (*kinako*). *Abekawa* (*A'bekawa*) is a river in *Shizuoka* City.
豊田 *Toyota*	クラウン最中	***kura'un monaka*** (Crown (car model) *monaka*) Two crisp *mochi*-based car-shaped wafers with *azuki* bean or other filling.
東大阪 *Higashi*	花ラグ饅頭	***hanaragu manjū*** *Manjū* in the shape of a bite-sized rugby ball, celebrating the area's long association with the game.
神戸 *Kōbe*	ゴーフル	***gōfuru*** (gaufre) A French-style waffle prepared with traditional *sembei* techniques. First developed in the 1920s.
福岡 *Fukuoka*	明太子	***menta'iko*** Cod roe often used in *ochazu'ke*, *onigiri* and spaghetti dishes.
大分 *Ōita*	ざびえる	***zabieru*** (Xavier) Butter biscuits named after St Francis Xavier, who brought Christianity to Japan in the 16th century
熊本 *Kumamoto*	辛子レンコン	***karashi renkon*** Fried lotus root with *miso* and *karashi* mustard. In the past most *Kumamoto* households prepared their own *karashi renkon* at New Year.

Talk of a fried lotus root souvenir brings us neatly to the end of your preparation for the Land of the Rising Sun.

We think you're ready. You can cheer on your team at the stadium, or even on the sofa. You can talk to complete strangers. You can handle restaurants, hotels, shops and bars. You've read Japanese words and can decipher potentially thousands more. You know when to take off your shoes and what not to do in the bath. Japan is waiting for you! .

Hontō-ni yoku yatta!
(You've really done well!)

Best of luck to you and your team!

Appendix 1: General vocabulary and phrases

Yes	*ha'i*
No	*ī'e*

Greetings	
Hello	*kon'nichi-wa*
Good evening	*konban-wa*
Good morning	*ohayō (goza'imasu)*
Nice to meet you (How do you do?)	*haji'me-mashi'te*
Good night	*oyasumi-nasa'i*
Good-bye	*sa'yonara*

Polite expressions	
Thank you	*arigatō*
I'm sorry	*sumima'sen*
Excuse me	*sumima'sen*
(Before eating food)	*itada'kimasu*
Thank you for the food	*gochisō-sama*

Communication	
I don't understand	*wakarima'sen*
Do you speak English?	*eigo dekimasu-ka?*

Questions	
Where is X? p. 12	*X wa doko desu ka?*
How much (is X?) p. 41	*(X wa) ikura desu ka?*
Do you have X? p. 134	*X arimasu ka?*
Is it okay?	*ii desu ka?*
Can I pay by card? p. 138	*kādo de ii desu ka?*

Is this the right queue? p. 68	*kono retsu de ii desu ka?*
Can I leave my luggage? p. 133	*nimotsu o azu'ke'te'mo ii desu ka?*
What floor is the room? p. 132	*heya wa nan-ka'i desu ka?*
What time (is breakfast) from? p. 133	*(chōshoku wa) nan-ji kara desu ka?*
Until what time? p. 133	*nan-ji ma'de desu ka?*

Statements	
I am... He/she/it is... They are... X p. 16/p. 18	*X desu*
I made a reservation p. 131	*yoyaku shimashita*
I want to go to X p. 68	*X ni ikita'i desu*
I don't want a bag p. 134	*fukuro wa ii desu*

Requests	
Excuse me!	*sumima'sen*
X please	*X kudasa'i (asking to receive an object)* *X o'nega'i shimasu*
Coffee, please	*kōhī kudasa'i*
Tōkyō Station, please	*Tōkyō eki o'nega'i shimasu*
No-smoking seats, please	*ki(n)'en seki o'nega'i shimasu*

For specific vocabulary, see the following pages:

Accommodation: p. 129–133
Country names: p. 17
Currencies: p. 41
Directions: p. 12/3
Drink: p. 125–128
Family/friends: p. 18
Food: p. 109–124

Money: p. 138–139
Numbers: p. 30–40
Possessions: p. 143
Problems: p. 141–142
Rugby: p. 20–24
Transport: p. 64–69

Appendix 2: Signs

Here are the wordings of some signs you're likely to see:

トイレ　お手洗い　便所　化粧室　lavatory

男　男子　紳士　殿方　men

女　女子　ご婦人　women

入口　entrance　出口　exit

非常口　emergency exit

非常階段　emergency staircase

押す　push　　　引く　pull

開　open (lift door)　閉　close (lift door)

営業中　open (shop/restaurant)

本日閉店　本日休業　準備中　three versions of 'closed'

営業時間　opening hours

工事中　men at work

危険　danger

立入禁止　do not enter

注意　caution

For some common emergency refuge signs, see p.144.

Appendix 3: Training/Miniquiz Answers

Warm-up 2

TO RA I = try   SU KU RA MU = scrum

Miniquiz 2
aka'i

Training 8 (c)
a) *go ta'i san*; b) *jū ta'i rei*; c) *hachi ta'i nana*; d) *rei ta'i roku*;
e) *kyū ta'i go*

Training 9
a) *san ta'i jū-nana*

c) *hachi ta'i jū-yon*

e) *jū-kyū ta'i rei*

b) *jū-roku ta'i jū*

d) *jū-go ta'i jū-ichi*

Training 10
a) *yon-jū ta'i jū-roku*

d) *san-jū-ni ta'i kyū*

b) *ni-jū-go ta'i nana*

e) *go-jū ta'i jū-go*

c) *san ta'i hachi-jū-hachi*

Miniquiz 3
Score in the 2015 World Cup Final: (b) *san-jū-yon ta'i jū-nana*
(New Zealand 34 Australia 17)

Miniquiz 4
Highest score by a team in a World Cup match:
(b) *hyaku-yon-jū-go* (145) by NZ against Japan (17) in 1995

Training 12
1. a) vii; b) iii; c) vi; d) ii; e) v; f) i; g) iv

2. a) *ichi-man-yon-sen-kyū-hyaku-en*; b) *nana-man-roku-sen-en*

Miniquiz 5
a) *ni-sen-jū-kyū-en* – 2,019 yen (adult); *sen-en* – 1,000 yen (child)
b) *jū-man-en* – 100,000 yen

Training 14
1) c) スクラム = *sukuramu* = scrum
   (Others: a) スカンク = *sukanku* = skunk; b) スキム = *sukimu* = skim)

2) b) **トライ** = *tora'i* = try.
(Others: a) **トレイ** = *torei* = tray; c) **トイレ** = *toi're* = toilet)

3) b) **ラインアウト** = *rainauto* = lineout

(Others: a) **ライムライト** = *ra'imura'ito* = limelight
c) **ラインラント** = *ra'inranto* = Rhineland – based on German pronunciation)

Training 15

a) **フランカー** = *furankā* = flanker

b) **フルバック** = *furubakku* = full-back

c) **フライハーフ** = *fura'ihāfu* = fly-half

d) **フッカー** = *fukkā* = hooker

e) **プロップ** = *puroppu* = prop

Training 16 (a)

a) **ジョナ・ロムー** *jona romū* = Jonah Lomu – most tries in World Cup matches (15) – shared with Bryan Habana.

b) **ギャビン・ヘイスティングス** *gyabin heisutingusu* = Gavin Hastings – most conversions in World Cup matches (39).

c) **ジョニー・ウィルキンソン** = *jonī wirukinson* = Johnny Wilkinson – most penalties (58), drop goals (14) and overall points in World Cup matches (277).

Training 16 (b)

a) *tonga*: Tonga – Pool C

b) *sukottorando*: Scotland – Pool A

c) *ōsutoraria*: Australia – Pool D

d) *kanada*: Canada – Pool B

Training 16 (c)

a) goal; b) touchline; c) touch judge; d) line-out; e) referee; f) ball

Appendix 4: *Katakana* Reading Key

The basic 45 symbols

Vowels	ア A	イ I	ウ U	エ E	オ O	
K	カ KA	キ KI	ク KU	ケ KE	コ KO	
S	サ SA	シ SHI	ス SU	セ SE	ソ SO	
T	タ TA	チ CHI	ツ TSU	テ TE	ト TO	
N	ナ NA	ニ NI	ヌ NU	ネ NE	ノ NO	Post-vocalic ン N
H	ハ HA	ヒ HI	フ FU	ヘ HE	ホ HO	
M	マ MA	ミ MI	ム MU	メ ME	モ MO	
Y	ヤ YA		ユ YU		ヨ YO	
R(L)	ラ RA	リ RI	ル RU	レ RE	ロ RO	
W	ワ WA					

Variations on the basic 45 symbols

1. **Two small strokes** (like speech marks) at top-right of characters. This changes the pronunciation as follows:
   K to G – for example: カ (KA) becomes ガ (GA)
   S to Z – for example: サ (SA) becomes ザ (ZA)
   SH to J – シ (SHI) becomes ジ (JI)
   T to D – for example: タ (TA) becomes ダ (DA)
   TS to Z – ツ (TSU) becomes ヅ (ZU)
   H to B – for example: ハ (HA) becomes バ (BA)
   U to VU – ウ (U) becomes ヴ (VU)

2. A **small circle** top-right of an H character changes the sound to P:
   For example: ハ (HA) becomes パ (PA)

3. A **long hyphen-like symbol** after any character lengthens the vowel:
   For example: ボ (BO) becomes ボー (BŌ) as in ボール (*bōru* = ball)

4. A **small ツ (TSU)** character signifies a short pause before the following consonant:
   For example: キック (KI (PAUSE) KU) (*kikku* = kick)

5. **Characters in small font** combine with the preceding full-sized character to produce different syllables as shown in the chart on the following page:

		アA	イI	ウU	エE	オO	ヤ YA	ユ YU	ヨ YO
SECOND CHARACTER (SMALL)									
FIRST CHARACTERR	ウ U		ウィ WI		ウェ WE	ウォ WO			
	ヴ VU	ヴァ VA	ヴィ VI		ヴェ VE	ヴォ VO			
	キ KI						キャ KYA	キュ KYU	キョ KYO
	ギ GI						ギャ GYA	ギュ GYU	ギョ GYO
	シ SHI				シェ SHE		シャ SHA	シュ SHU	ショ SHO
	ジ JI				ジェ JE		ジャ JA	ジュ JU	ジョ JO
	チ CHI				チェ CHE		チャ CHA	チュ CHU	チョ CHO
	テ TE		ティ TI					テュ TYU	
	デ DE		ディ DI					デュ DYU	
	ト TO			トゥ TU					
	ド DO			ドゥ DU					
	ニ NI						ニャ NYA	ニュ NYU	ニョ NYO
	ヒ HI						ヒャ HYA	ヒュ HYU	ヒョ HYO
	ビ BI						ビャ BYA	ビュ BYU	ビョ BYO
	フ FU	ファ FA	フィ FI		フェ FE	フォ FO			
	ピ PI						ピャ PYA	ピュ PYU	ピョ PYO
	ミ MI						ミャ MYA	ミュ MYU	ミョ MYO
	リ RI						リャ RYA	リュ RYU	リョ RYO

154

Notes

Notes

Notes

Notes

Notes

WORLD RUGBY MUSEUM

TWICKENHAM
STADIUM TOURS

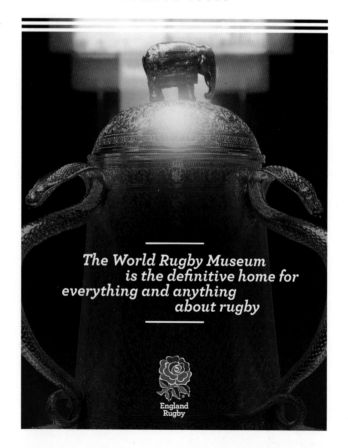

*The World Rugby Museum
is the definitive home for
everything and anything
about rugby*

England
Rugby